The
Copenhaver
Family

in the
Revolutionary War

Written and Compiled by
Richard L. Thayer

HERITAGE BOOKS
2006

HERITAGE BOOKS

AN IMPRINT OF HERITAGE BOOKS, INC.

Books, CDs, and more—Worldwide

For our listing of thousands of titles see our website
at
www.HeritageBooks.com

Published 2006 by
HERITAGE BOOKS, INC.
Publishing Division
65 East Main Street
Westminster, Maryland 21157-5026

International Standard Book Number: 978-0-7884-1949-8

DEDICATION

This publication is dedicated to all the descendants of Johann Wolfgang Koppenhoffer, our oldest immigrant ancestor, to promote a better understanding and appreciation of the early Copenhaver family members and their place in history.

FOREWORD

History is biased by the information that survives, and so, this publication will contain only part of the story of the Copenhaver Family in the Revolutionary War. This story will be biased by what recorded information survived the years and what part of that information I was able to find. It is not my intent to glorify anyone or to neglect anyone. I have presented the information as I found it.

I apologize for any recorded historical fact that has been missed or any printed error that will elude my detection and be repeated here.

I hope that this book will serve at least two purposes. One, to better inform all who are interested in the participation of the Copenhaver Family in the Revolutionary War and second to encourage others to search for what I have missed.

It was my intention when I started this book to document the military service in the American Revolution of every member of the Copenhaver Family who was a descendant of Wolfgang Koppenheffer.

This book has been limited in scope to direct descendants of Wolfgang Koppenheffer and their spouses, with one exception. One Koppenheffer line is included which is not related to Wolfgang (at least not closely related). The family of Joh. Jacob Copenhaver is included because of the military service of Jacob and to show where he does or does not properly fit in the family tree.

I have included some information on the Mossers, Hetricks and other collateral families, but only because they actually saw military service with the Copenhavers. I will leave a detailed study of the military service of these other families for another time.

The Copenhaver family had lived in Pennsylvania for 46 years before the start of the Revolutionary War. They had come to North America from Germany in 1728 to live in Penn's Colony, which was established to accept immigrants who were seeking religious freedom and a more prosperous life. Economic conditions had been bad in the Palatine District of Germany for years and many families had moved from that area. It is apparent that the Copenhaver Family found what they were seeking in North America because when their new-found freedom and way of life were threatened by England, many members of the family joined the patriot cause.

The first Copenhaver immigrants settled on what was then the western frontier of Pennsylvania in Lancaster County and took up farming on land that was acquired from the sons of William Penn. Civilization was continually pushing the frontier westward, but even during the French and Indian War in the 1750's it was not unusual for the inhabitants of Lancaster County to suffer at the hands of raiding Indians. As far as I can determine no Copenhavers were killed during these raids, but their neighbors and inlaws were not always so fortunate.

It was this background of a harsh frontier life and newly acquired economic and religious freedom which made the Copenhaver Family able and willing to help support the patriot cause in the Revolutionary War. At least 14 men with the name Copenhaver fought during the war. Numerous cousins, nephews, and inlaws of the Copenhaver family also served during the war. One female, Rosina Kucher Orth, is credited with patriotic service by the Daughters of the American Revolution.

In most cases the service of the men was intermittent enlistments in the local militia units. These militia units were called into active service to perform garrison duty, guard prisoners and to assist the Continental Army during major campaigns. In some campaigns of the war the militia contributed a high proportion of the men engaged as well as contributing a fighting spirit equivalent to the regular army.

ACKNOWLEDGMENTS

I have received much unselfish help with this work from numerous family members and others who enjoy history and genealogy. I cannot name everyone but I shall name some individuals, for their assistance was particularly noteworthy:

Clifford R. Canfield, for his Copenhaver genealogy written in 1958, was my introduction and inspiration to genealogical research.

Viola Kohl Mohn, for her contribution of genealogical and local history from the Myerstown, area where the early American Copenhavers lived.

Mildred M. Copenhaver, formerly of Joppa, Maryland, for her fine example of a written family history and a close-knit family through reunions, correspondence and a family newsletter.

Cornelius E. Koppenheffer, for his extensive knowledge of all branches of the Copenhaver family and his detailed information concerning their military service.

v

NAME SPELLING VARIATIONS

For the sake of continuity the Copenhaver name will be spelled only one way throughout the text of this publication, but the name will be spelled as it appears in original documents when they are reproduced. For the sake of historical accuracy I will discuss the variations of spelling that have occurred in the past.

The first Copenhaver immigrants who came from Germany to North America in 1728 and 1732 spelled the name Koppenhoffer. They could not speak English, but spoke and wrote only German. This is evidenced by the fact that even second and third generation American Copenhavers still wrote in German. Captain Thomas Copenhaver, of the third generation had to issue orders to his troops in German during the Revolutionary War because some privates under his command understood only German.

An interesting picture can be imagined as we visualize English and German being spoken by participants on both sides during the war. There were numerous instances where German speaking Pennsylvania troops fought against German "Hessian" Mercenaries.

As the name Copenhaver began to be Anglicized we see variations written as: Kopenheffer, Coppenhaver, Kopenhaver and Coppenheaver. Some of these transitional spellings are due to problems of translation from German to English and some spellings are due to a low level of spelling ability of the person writing the record. Excerpts from census records, church records and legal documents give us these variations of spelling: Copanhafer,

Copenheifer, Cuppenheifer, Cuppehefer, Cuppeheeffer and Cuppyheffer. Due to the depth and accuracy of the research performed by other family members on the Copenhaver genealogy we can now determine where these various people fit into the family.

Contents

LIST OF APPENDICES

CHAPTER 1

MATHIAS SMYSER (SCHMEISSER)

Mathias Smyser was born in Germany in 1715 and was the oldest Copenhaver in-law to serve in the Revolutionary War. He married Anna Catherine Copenhaver, youngest daughter of Wolfgang Copenhaver, in 1738 and was the only member of the second generation for whom I can document military service. The following paragraphs describing his Revolutionary War service were taken from "History of the Smyser Family in America 1731 - 1831."

Mathias Smyser was in the Revolutionary War, not as a soldier but as a teamster conducting a baggage wagon, when York Co. was called to provide 118 wagons for the purpose of removing government stores to places of safety, west of the Susquehanna River. This occurred shortly after the battle of Germantown [Oct. 4, 1777].

Mathias Smyser was a zealous advocate of the American cause, and so were all of his [11] children. Mathias Emerick Smyser and his brother, Jacob Mathias Smyser, were privates in Captain Emanuel Herman's company in 1777 and belonged to the second battalion (Prowell's History of York Co., Page 273-175).

John Michael Smyser, the only other child of Mathias and Anna Catherine to serve in the war, has a very extensive and active military record which will be discussed further in Chapter 15.

Mathias Smyser died on April 12, 1778 and is listed in "Known Military Dead During the American

1

Revolutionary War 1775-1783." Even though it is obvious that he died during the war, there is no indication that his death was battle related or even attributable to the rigors of military service. Since he was 63 years old at the time, it is possible that he died of natural causes or illness not related to his military service in 1777.

CHAPTER 2

HEINRICH COPENHAVER

Heinrich Copenhaver signed the Oath of allegiance to the patriot cause on June 22, 1778. He was forty-eight years old at the time. (Pennsylvania Archives, Series 2, Volume 13, Page 425). In 1781 he was in the Fifth Class of Captain Wendel Weavers' 7th Company of the Second Battalion of Lancaster County Militia. He was 52 years old at the time and was listed as "above age." (Pennsylvania Archives, Series 5, Volume 7, Page 161).

Heinrich Copenhaver was apparently not very active in the war due to his age.

CHAPTER 3

MICHAEL COPENHAVER

The military service of Michael Copenhaver is very sketchy. Cornelius Koppenheffer in an article in "Pennsylvania Dutchman" on November 15, 1950 says that Michael Copenhaver was a signer of the "Remonstrance of Berks County" in 1779 and that he served as a private in Captain Battorf's Company from Bethel Township, Berks County. No other information has been found for Michael Copenhaver.

CHAPTER 4

CAPTAIN SIMON COPENHAVER

Simon Copenhaver was living in Heidelberg Township, now Lebanon County, Pennsylvania in 1768 where he bought a house from Tobias Bickel. Sometime between 1768 and 1774 he moved with his family to York County where he acquired a farm. On December 16, 1774 Simon Copenhaver was voted a member of the York County Ruling Committee, also known as the Committee of Safety and the Committee of Observation. (Pennsylvania Archives Series 2, Volume 14, Page 493, also Prowell Volume I, Page 243). He apparently served in this capacity during 1775. Sometime in 1776 he served as a captain in the 1st Battalion of the York County Militia. (Pennsylvania Archives, Series 6, Volume 2, Page 420).

From October 1, 1777 to April 5, 1778 Simon Copenhaver held the commission of Captain in the Third company of the Second Battalion of York County Militia under Colonel William Rankin. Two muster rolls reproduced as Appendix "P" and "Q" show the size of his company and the extreme German character of this group of men. It cannot be determined whether this company was on guard duty at Camp Security guarding the prisoners from Burgoyne's surrender at Saratoga on October 17, 1777. Some D.A.R. sources say that this was the case but no contemporary documents have been found to support this conclusion. Other D.A.R. and S.A.R. sources say that during the winter of 1778 the horses of General Washington and his staff were kept at the farm of Captain Simon Copenhaver near York. No evidence of this event has been found.

From the pension application of Thomas Wilt (W3322 Appendix "T") we learn that he served under Captain Simon Copenhaver for two months during the fall of 1778 guarding prisoners from Burgoyne's surrender at Saratoga. This presumably occurred at Camp Security. Valentine Wilt was probably the father of Thomas Wilt. From the D.A.R. lineage book Volume 84, Page 193 we learn that Valentine Wilt served from 1776 to 1779 as a private in Captain Simon Copenhaver's Company. He is also listed as belonging to the 6th class York County Militia on February 5, 1782. Valentine Wilt died in 1796 in York. As of the time of this writing no other pension applicants who served under Captain Simon Copenhaver have been found.

Captain Simon Copenhaver served at Camp Security from August 10, 1781 until October 10, 1781. His name appears on the voucher book of William Scott, pp. 10-12. (National Archives Film No. 1205979). The muster roll of Captain Copenhaver and the payroll for the company during this period are listed in Appendix "R".

Further information on the service of Captain Copenhaver's Company at Camp Security is found in the following document reproduced from the Pennsylvania Archives, Series 6, Volume 2, Page 777.

"Camp Security, September 29, 1781 the bearer Mich'l Miller is discharged from this camp as he faithfully served his tower in the militia."

John Mapping, Lieut.

"I do hereby certify the bearer Fredk. Youse Junier to receive all my pay or payment of a tour of duty in the Fourth class at Camb Securety for carting the British prisoners of ware in Captain Copenhavers Compony. I do hereby give power said Fredk. Youse for all such pay at all pleses paymaster or county leughtennant for value recd. as witness my hand and seal this 10th day of February 1784."

Michael Miller. (Seal.)

Witness Present

Johannes Brenckman

Another muster roll of Captain Copenhaver's Company appears in Appendix "O". It bears the date February 5, 1782 at the beginning of the document and the date February 8, 1783 at the end of the document. I have no explanation of this apparent discrepancy. This muster roll is published in two different places; Pennsylvania Archives, Series 6, Volume 2, Pages 655-657, and Henry Young, Red Series, Volume 1, Pages 68-72. There is no source to show what military activity might have been performed by the company during this period.

In October of 1783 Captain Simon Copenhaver was a signer on a petition sent to John Dickinson, Esq., President of the Supreme Executive Council of the Commonwealth of Pennsylvania, to keep the militia quartered at Yorktown, for the protection of the people of York County, (C.E. Koppenheffer, "Pennsylvania Dutchman" 1950).

More details can probably be found concerning the service of Captain Simon Copenhaver with a more diligent search of the pension application records for the names of men on the various muster rolls.

CHAPTER 5

CAPTAIN THOMAS COPENHAVER

Of the family members discussed here Captain Thomas Copenhaver was the most prominent participant in the war. His active service was almost continuous from 1775 to 1779. This service spans all of the major activity in the North during the war.

Captain Thomas Copenhaver was 35 years old when he participated in the drafting, and was one of the nine signers, of the Hanover Resolutions (Appendix K) on June 4, 1774. It is interesting to note that Captain Thomas Copenhaver and Colonel Timothy Green were the only persons of German background to sign the document. Based on their names, the other seven men had predominantly Scotch-Irish or English backgrounds. The Resolutions were apparently drafted and signed at Harpers Inn in Harpers, Lancaster County, now Lebanon County, Pennsylvania. (Koppenheffer, Cornelius E., personal communication 1984). Captain Thomas Copenhaver would later serve in campaigns with Colonel Timothy Green and Colonel John Rogers. These men would soon be active in the formation of the Lancaster County Associators, the basis of the Pennsylvania Militia. The Hanover Resolutions predate the Suffolk Resolves and other similar documents and it is evident that the basic grievances and resolutions that are expressed in these early documents were later restated in a more thorough and eloquent form in the Declaration of Independence.

On November 22, 1774, and probably before, handbills were posted and circulated in Lancaster County calling for volunteers to the patriot cause (Mohn, Viola K., personal communication 1984). In response to this call Captain Thomas Copenhaver raised a company of riflemen in East Hanover Township, Lancaster County, now Lebanon County, Pennsylvania. This company was in The Hanover Rifle Battalion under the command of Colonel Timothy Green of the Lancaster County Associators. (Egle, William H., History of the Counties of Dauphin and Lebanon 1883). Apparently the first action seen by these militia associators occurred in the fall of 1775. They were called to arms in response to the British activity in and around New York City. Two men who were under the command of Captain Thomas Copenhaver during this time told of their recollections in pension applications almost 57 years later. John Harkerader who was a lieutenant and William Hedrick who was a fifer were both in this campaign. (Harkerader, John; Pension Application S13323, Appendix F; Hedrick, William; Pension Application R4355 Appendix H). Although the passage of time and their advanced age had made their memories a bit hazy the story can be pieced together as follows: Captain Thomas Copenhaver commanded a company of riflemen in the second battalion of the Lancaster County Associators. The colonel was Timothy Green and Abraham Latcha was the major. There were probably from 60 to 80 privates and subordinate officers, each was provided with a blanket and rifle supplied by the Associator organization. (Gerbrich, John; Pension Application S22122, Appendix E). The rifles that each man carried were manufactured by local gunsmiths in Lancaster and neighboring counties. These rifles could be shot with good accuracy up to 200 yards due to the recent development of rifled or grooved barrels. A large number of these rifles survive to this day and they are fine examples of early American craftsmanship.

The company marched first to Philadelphia from their point of rendezvous in Lancaster County, a distance of about 100 miles. They then marched North through Elizabeth Town (probably in New Jersey) to Perth Amboy, New Jersey - then to Bergen Town, New Jersey which was directly across the Hudson River from New York City. Presumably it was near here that they participated in a battle with the British in which the Patriot forces were defeated. William Hedrick mentions this battle but gives us no details. This could not have been a major battle for two reasons: first, had it been a major engagement it would have been better remembered by William Hedrick and John Harkerader, and second, I can find no record of any major battles in this area at that time.

After the battle they marched back to Trenton, New Jersey and then back to Lancaster County where they disbanded and returned to their homes. There is some confusion about the duration of their service during this campaign. John Harkerader says it was from August 1, 1775 to October 1, 1775, a period of two months. William Hedrick says it was six months from the fall of 1775 until the spring of 1776.

The next period of military activity for Captain Thomas Copenhaver is a three month campaign in the summer of 1776 under Colonel Philip L. Greenawalt and Major Abraham Latcha. This information was gathered from the pension applications of John Hoover and Peter Breakbill Jr., privates who served under Captain Thomas Copenhaver. John Hoover states that the company "was at Paulus Hook when the British frigates lay at New York bay." (Hoover, John; Pension Application S4402, Appendix I). No mention is made of any infantry engagement with the British during this campaign nor of the route taken on the way home from Paulus Hook.

Peter Breakbill went into service in July 1776 as a substitute for his brother Phillip Breakbill who was drafted for three months.

Captain Copenhaver's company marched first to Philadelphia from Lancaster County, where they remained in barracks three or four weeks. "The Barracks (enclosing four acres with brick) were full of men," but Peter Breakbill could not remember the name of the commanding officer. (Breakbill, Peter; Pension Application W-46, Appendix M). The company then went up the Delaware River in a schooner to Trenton, New Jersey, stayed there one day, then marched on towards New York. They accompanied a large army of militia on this march. They marched to Bergen Town, New Jersey and then to Paulus Hook, New Jersey across the Hudson River from New York City. The company stayed at Paulus Hook until the three month term of service expired.

During their stay at Paulus Hook, Peter Breakbill says that "The British were piping up the North River with the Roebuck and two other ships cannonaded the fort which fire the fort returned."

The activities of Captain Thomas Copenhaver during the fall of 1776 are in doubt, not because of a lack of information, but because of too much conflicting information. On August 12, 1776 the company of Captain Copenhaver was mustered in Lancaster as part of Colonel Timothy Greens' battalion of militia. The other officers were Lieutenant Colonel Peter Hedrick, First Major John Rogers and Second Major Abraham Latcha. The Muster Roll published in the Pennsylvania Archives Series 5 Volume 7 also shows Lieutentant John Harkerader, fifer William Hedrick and privates John Hoover (Huber) and Peter Breakbill. It is indicated that the company was active until January or February 1777.

On August 19, 1776 the Pennsylvania Council of Safety voted to direct Mr. Robert Towers to deliver to Captain Copenhaver of Colonel Timothy Green's Battalion, three muskets and take his receipt.

The following accounts were passed, and Mr. Nesbitt directed to pay them, and charge the same to Congress, viz:

... Captain Coppenhaven's Comp'y, Col. Green's
Battalion   Lancaster County, £4 15s

(Minutes of the Council of Safety, Pennsylvania Archives, Colonial Records, Volume 10, Page 691-692).
Doctor Egle says that Captain Copenhaver and company were in the battle of Long Island on August 27, 1776 and were also in the terrible retreat across the Jerseys.

(Egle, William H.; History of the Counties of Dauphin and Lebanon 1883). I have found no supporting information which indicates that this is true. It seems that the pension applicants would remember this. H.M.M. Richards reports that Captain Copenhaver and his company went to the front under Colonel Timothy Green after the Battle of Long Island but he offers no documentation for this statement. (Richards, Captain H.M.M.; Lebanon County's Part in the Revolutionary War 1909).

Doctor Egle says that Captain Copenhaver and his company were surrendered at Fort Washington but paroled and sent home. While I have found this to be true of some other Pennsylvania militia companies I have not found any documentation that would support this statement.

Peter Breakbill states in his pension application that in November 1776 he went into service as a substitute for his Uncle Peter Breakbill, who was drafted for a term of three months. He marched under Captain Thomas Copenhaver and Major Abraham Latcha as he did beforehand with Peter Hedrick as colonel. This statement conflicts with the Muster Roll published in the Pennsylvania archives (Appendix A) which shows Timothy Green as colonel and Peter Hedrick as lieutenant colonel. Peter Brightbill appears as first lieutenant and another Peter Brightbill appears as a private on the roll. It is possible that this is not a conflict since the Muster Roll is dated August 12, 1776 and he could be referring to another 3 month tour of duty immediately following the first.

During this tour Peter Breakbill states that they marched from said Lebanon (Lancaster) County to Readingtown, thence Ellentown . . . Brunswick in New Jersey, remaining there a week or more, from Brunswich they were ordered back to Trenton. There they joined a large body of militia and the flying camp. They took a large number of Hessian prisoners (perhaps 1,500) and marched them to Lancaster and guarded them in the barracks until his 3 month term of service expired.

The way Peter Breakbill has worded his statement leaves me in doubt about his participation in the Battle of

15

Trenton, but I presume that he was not in the battle or else he would have been more definite about his statements. It is obvious though, that Captain Copenhaver's company escorted the Hessian prisoners captured during the Battle of Trenton to the Lancaster Barracks for their confinement.

The next documented activity of Captain Copenhaver comes from the pension application of John Bickel. (Also Pickel and Beackel). (Bickel, John; Pension Application S22122 Appendix E). John Bickel was possibly the son of Tobias Bickel and close neighbor of Captain Thomas Copenhaver. In 1768 Simon Copenhaver (brother to Captain Thomas Copenhaver) bought the Tobias Bickel house in Myerstown, Pennsylvania and in later years some of the Bickel family moved to Virginia with the family of Captain Thomas Copenhaver. It seems likely that John Bickel's recollections of Captain Thomas Copenhaver would be accurate.

John Bickel states that he served under Captain Copenhaver from January 2, 1777 until March 2, 1777 during which time the company "marched from Jonestown (now Lebanon County, Pennsylvania) to Philadelphia, to Trenton, New Jersey to Princeton, to Rockyhill, New Jersey and then back to Princeton." It is possible that the general headquarters for Washington's army was near Rocky Hill, New Jersey during this time. John states that the company was discharged by General Israel Putnam at Princeton and the men returned home from there.

It is likely that this company was in the second battalion of Lancaster County militia because a document dated March 18, 1777 reads:

"Mr. Nesbitt directed to pay Captain T. Kopenhaver 445 pounds for blankets appraised for the use of the second battalion of Lancaster Militia to be charged for Congress." (Egle, William H.; Pennsylvania archives Series 2 Volume 1). This document also stated that they were absent in the Jerseys until June 1777. This is in conflict with what John Bickel has stated.

On January 31, 1777 the Council of Safety passed the following resolution, "An order was drawn on Mr.

Nesbitt in favor of Major Latcha for one month's pay of 2 companies of Col. Tim'y Green's Batt'n of Lancaster County, viz: Captains Ropenhever (sic) and Stoner - 2 captains, 3 lieut'nants, 5 sergeants, 4 drummers and fifers, 44 privates."

The fall of 1777 is another period of activity of Captain Copenhaver in the patriot cause where the documentation is conflicting.

On July 31, 1777 Captain Copenhaver was commissioned captain of the first company of the sixth battalion of Lancaster County militia. (Pennsylvania Historical and Museum Commission). This battalion was commanded by Colonel John Rogers and Lieutenant Colonel Robert Clark. This is surely the same John Rogers who signed the Hanover Resolutions. We find reference again in the Pennsylvania Archives Series 5 Volume 7 that says Captain Copenhaver was commissioned Captain of the third company of 88 men in the 6th battalion of Lancaster County militia commanded by Colonel John Rogers and Lieutenant Colonel Robert Clark. There is also mention of Ensign John Beackle (Bickle).

The conflicting information to the previously cited military service comes from the published Pennsylvania archives and battalion returns in the possession of the Pennsylvania Historical and Museum Commission in Harrisburg. On August 18, 1777 Captain Copenhaver is reported to be stationed at Chester, Pennsylvania under the command of Colonel Alexander Lowery. The Pennsylvania Archives state that, on August 30, 1777, Captain Copenhaver's company is part of the third Battalion of Lancaster County militia stationed at Chester, Pennsylvania under Colonel Alexander Lowery. On August 3, 1777 Col. Galbraith in a letter to Col. Rogers states ... "to march without loss of time the first, second and third class of your battalion to Chester on Delaware". While it is obvious that Captain Copenhaver was very active in the war during August of 1777, I know of no way to sort out this conflicting information.

On May 9, 1778 Captain Thomas Copenhaver's name appears on an oath of allegiance to the patriot cause.

17

The oath was administered by Colonel Timothy Green. From April 24, 1778 until October 28, 1779 Captain Thomas Copenhaver was on the Muster Roll as captain of the Third Company of the Sixth Battalion of the Lancaster County Militia. The Muster Roll states, however, that he did not serve, having no command. (Pennsylvania Archives 5th Series, Volume 7, Pages 545-547, Appendix L). Although the war in the North was not over and some battles were still fought in 1778-1780 there is no documentation to indicate that Captain Thomas Copenhaver was active in the war during that period.

It is probable that the house that the Thomas Copenhaver family lived in during the Revolutionary is Building #955 on the Fort Indiantown Gap Military Reservation northeast of Lebanon, Pennsylvania.

Early in 1780 Captain Thomas Copenhaver moved with most of his children and their spouses to the town of Crocket in Wythe County, Virginia. There is no indication that Captain Thomas Copenhaver participated in the war while he lived in Virginia.

Captain Thomas Copenhaver died in Virginia in 1802 at the age of 63. Unfortunately he did not live long enough to apply for a pension for his military service. He could have clarified and answered many questions about his military service.

CHAPTER 6

JOHN TICE

John Tice (also Teis and Teise) is listed as a private in the Fourth Class of Captain Wendel Weaver's 7th Company of the 2nd Battalion of the Lancaster County Militia in both 1781 and 1782. Both references are in Pennsylvania Archives, Series 5, Volume 7, Pages 161 and 182. The 1782 company return is dated July 8th and is signed by John Gloninger, Sub-lieutenant of Lancaster County. No other sources of information have been found.

CHAPTER 7

CHRISTIAN LEHMAN III

Christian Lehman III is listed as a private in the 8th Class of Captain Wendel Weaver's 7th Company of the Second Battalion of Lancaster County Militia on July 8, 1782. (Pennsylvania Archives, Series 5, Volume 7, Page 183.) On his tombstone in Union Cemetery in Myerstown he is listed as being in the 8th Company of the 2nd Battalion of Lancaster County Militia. He may have served in 2 different companies or there may be confusion by his assignment to the 8th Class rather than 8th Company.

There is a pension file R6084 with the name of Christian Lehman as the claimant but this is a different individual from York County.

CHAPTER 8

CHRISTOPHER COPENHAVER, SR.

Christopher Copenhaver signed the following document January 2, 1781:
> "The State of Pennsylvania
>> To Christof. Coppenhaver -
>
> To 7 Bu. Rye @ 5/8 State £ 1.19.8
>> Rec. January 2d, 1781 of P. Marstellar one pound nineteen shillings and eight pence state money in full for the above rye.
>> Christof. Koppenhaver"

On July 8, 1782 he is listed as a private in the 8th Class of Captain Wendel Weaver's 7th Company of the Second Battalion of Lancaster County Militia. This company return is attested to by John Gloninger, Sub-lieutenant of Lancaster County. (Pennsylvania Archives, Series 7, Volume 2, Page 183).

Cornelius Koppenheffer in a 1984 letter stated that Christopher Copenhaver, Sr. was in the 8th Class of Heidelberg Township on June 22, 1778 but I cannot find any documentation to support this.

CHAPTER 9

JOHANN MICHAEL COPENHAVER, JR.

      Johann Michael Copenhaver, Jr. is listed in the D.A.R. Patriot Index as being a private from Pennsylvania. On May 22, 1777 he signed an Oath of Allegiance in the presence of T. Mayhill. (Mayhill L404B). No other references to his military service have been found.

CHAPTER 10

ADAM ORTH

As early as 1769 Adam Orth was a commissioner of the County of Lancaster. Adam Orth later assisted in the organization of the Associator Battalions of Lancaster County. On March 12, 1777 he was appointed Sub-lieutenant of Lancaster County and possibly served in that capacity until 1782. (Unpublished documents pertaining to Lebanon County's part in the War of the Revolution, Shenk, 1916). Some sources refer to "Colonel" Adam Orth but I can find no documentation for his commission. On May 1, 1778 Adam Orth and Christopher Kucher made a trip from Lebanon to Philadelphia as representatives of the Hebron congregation, "To tell the authorities how Major Watkins had filled, with powder, the residence portion of their church, occupied by the Reverend Bader, and praying for relief. On May 4, 1778 the Board of War directed the powder to be removed, and other stores put in its place." (Pennsylvania German in the Revolutionary War, Richards H.M.M., Page 509). "A list of certificates issued in the month of June 1780, by Philip Marsteller of Lancaster County in pay for cattle procured for the use of the Continental Army in pursuance of an Act of General Assembly on the 1st of June, 1780 and also of the several orders granted on the Honorable the Supreme Executive Council of the State of Pennsylvania.

Date of Certificate	Name of Person to Whom Cert. were granted	No. of Cert.	No.of Cattle	Amt. of Pounds	Amt. of Dollers
June 20, 1780	Col. Adam Orth	1	11	4572.10	11660
June 15, 1780	Baltzer Orth	11	1	620	693 1-3

"I do hereby certify that the foregoing is a just and true account of 84 head of beef cattle by me purchased and procured and delivered to Ephraim Blaine Esqr. Commg. of purchases for the use of the Contl. Army in the month of June 1780 amounting inclusive of every expenditure whatsoever save a reasonable compensation of my services and trouble to the sum £34 144.7.6 equal to 91051 2-3 dollars. Together with shewing the manner the said cattle were settled for as witness my hand this 3rd July, 1780.

P. Marsteller"

(Shenk, Ibid)

Adam Orth to President Reid

Lebanon, Aug. 18, 1780

"Sir:
I have lately recd. an appointment from Col. Attle Lieutenant of Lancaster County for the collection of the militia fines of said county due and payable in consequence of the late law — — many of the people in this part of the country think it a poor satisfaction to collect the said fines nominally, as the money is so much depreciated, but as I can hear of no law to enable me to demand the depreciation, I think it may duty to crave the opinion of the Honorable Council thereon — — I shall use my utmost endeavors to bring the business to a close as soon as possibly may be — And do myself the honor of subscribing my self.

Your Exl. Very Hum Servt.

Adam Orth

P.S. - An early answer
would be very acceptable.
A.O.

Jos. Reid, Esqr. Prendt."
(Shenk, Ibid)

In 1789 and 1790 Adam Orth was Dauphin County's representative to the Pennsylvania General Assembly. (Pennsylvania Genealogies, Egle, W.H., 1886) Adam Orth died in 1794 at the age of 61. He is buried in the Hebron Moravian Graveyard at Lebanon, Pennsylvania. His tombstone inscription says that he was in the First company of the 2nd Battalion of the Lancaster County Militia. (Revolutionary war soldiers buried in Lebanon County, Weaver, C.E., 1976). I can find no other reference to the military service of Adam Orth in the First Company of the 2nd Battalion or any other Lancaster County unit.

CHAPTER 11

CHRISTOPHER KUCHER

The activities of Christopher Kucher during the Revolutionary War were more oriented towards public service and administration rather than military service. I have found reference to his enlistment at Salem Church, but I cannot determine when this occurred or what organization he joined. It was probably early in the war. (Development of East Lebanon, PA, Page 183)

In 1778 Christopher Kucher and Adam Orth were sent by the congregation of the Moravian Church to the Board of War at York, Pennsylvania to petition for the removal of powder stored in the church. The ammunition was removed May 4, 1778 and less dangerous supplies were stored in the church. (Lebanon County's part in the Rvolutionary War, Page 400)

Sometime in 1778 or 1779 Christopher Kucher was paid for forage furnished to the magazine at Lebanon, Lebanon County, Pennsylvania. (National Genealogical Society Quarterly, Volume XXVI,No. 3, 1928)

In June of 1780 Christopher Kucher was carrying on an active correspondence with President Reed and the Supreme Executive Council concerning various affairs of the Pennsylvania Militia. In one letter he signs off as S.L.L.C. which stands for Sub-Lieutenant Lancaster County and has the title of colonel. (Appendix "Y")

Christopher Kucher received depreciation pay as a private for service in the Lancaster County Militia. (Pennsylvania Archives, Series 5, Volume 4, Page 309)

As further proof of his rank and title Christopher Kucher signed the discharge for George Henning.

CHAPTER 12

ROSINA KUCHER ORTH

Rosina Kucher Orth is one of the few women listed in the D.A.R. Patriot Index. She is a attributed with patriotic service during the Revolutionary War. The following biographical note about her was written by William H. Egle and appeared in print in two of his publications. The first was "Notes and Queries" Series 4, Volume I, Page 292 and the second was, "Some Pennsylvania Women During The War of The Revolution," published in Harrisburg in 1898.

Rosina Kucher, second daughter of Peter and Barbara Kucher, was born in Lebanon township, then Lancaster County, Pennsylvania, March 19, 1741. Her parents emigrated from the Palatinate, Germany, about the year 1737, and settled in Pennsylvania, where most of their large family of children were born. Educated under the care of the Moravian minister of the neighborhood, together with the instruction and example of a truly pious mother, Rosina became a woman of more than ordinary culture.

On the 26th of April, 1763, in Hebron Church, near Lebanon, she was married by Rev. Zahm, to Balzer Orth, also a native of the locality, where he was born July 14, 1736. His father, of the same name, came from the Palatinate, Germany, to Pennsylvania in 1730, where in 1735 he had warranted to him three hundred acres of land, on which he had been some time settled. The son was a man of prominence during the Revolutionary period, had served in the Bouquet expedition against the Ohio Indians in 1764, and early espoused the cause of the colonies in their struggle for independence. He was an officer in one of the associated battalions of Lancaster County, and after the victory at Trenton was in command of the company which was directed to guard the Hessian prisoners of war, confined at Lebanon. He was commissioned major of the Second Battalion, Colonel Greenawalt, August 26, 1780, and was in active service that year guarding the frontier settlers while gathering their crops, owing to the numerous marauds of the Indians from the northern lakes.

During this period Mrs. Orth was not a disinterested witness of transpiring events. True to her matronly duties, as well as the patriotic inspiration of the times, no one was more diligent in laboring for the relief of the American soldiery. Skilled in spinning and weaving, an accomplishment in which she justly prided herself, large quantities of clothing material were sent by her to the badly clothed men of the army of the Declaration. To her, and others of her neighbors (she was but one of the many), too great honor cannot be rendered, and it is only proper that their descendants cherish the patriotic self-devotion of these mothers of the Republic. Major Orth died October 6, 1794, his wife surviving until April 3, 1814. Both lie interred in Hebron church yard, near Lebanon. Of their eight children who reached maturity, the eldest son, Gottlieb, was the father of Hon. Godlove S. Orth, the famous Indiana statesman; while their eldest daughter, Maria-Barbara, was the maternal ancestor of the distinguished surgion, Prof. S.J. Jones, M.D., LL.D., of Chicago.

CHAPTER 13

BALTHASER ORTH

As early as July 14, 1776 militia companies were drilling in Balthaser Orth's field. The diary from the Hebron Moravian Church which was just opposite the field says, "The battalion recieved positive orders not to march out until after the public divine worship of the brethren, who were not to be disturbed, was ended." (The development of East Lebanon Page 186)

Balthaser Orth also assisted with guarding the Hessian prisoners who were taken at Trenton, N.J. on December 26, 1776, but no details of this event are known. (Notes and queries Series 4, Volume 1, Page 292)

In 1778 or 1779 Balthaser Orth was paid for forage furnished to the magazine at Lebanon, Pennsylvania. (National Genealogical society Quarterly, volume 16, No. 3, Page 43)

Captain Balthaser Orth was commanding the first company of the 2nd Battalion of the Lancaster County Militia on May 6, 1780. He served under Lt. Colonel Thomas Edwards and Major Valentine Shouffler. (Lebanon County's part in the Revolutionary War, Page 395) On June 15, 1780 Balthaser Orth sold a cow for the use of the Continental Army. He was paid £620 on Certificate No. 11 by P. Marsteller. (Unpublished documents pertaining to Lebanon County — Page 48)

Balthaser Orth was a major in the second battalion of Lancaster County Militia under Colonel Greenawalt on

August 26, 1780 when he was guarding against Indian attacks for 1 year according to Notes and Queries, Series 4, Volume 1, but this does not fit with subsequent information which shows him again as a captain in October and November of 1780. In grand account #CCLXXIII Ledger CP. 135 he is shown as receiving pay of £19213.15.0 as a Captain of Lancaster County Militia for October and November 1780. (National Archives Film No. 1205979)

By April 15, 1783 he had attained the rank of major of the 2nd Battalion Lancaster County Militia under Lt. Colonel John Gloninger. He still held this position on January 25, 1786 when he signed the following document:
"I do certify that Paul Sieg has regularly attended my company from the years 1777 to the spring of the year 1783 and behaved himself as a good militia man during the time aforesaid."
To Col. John Gloninger

Balthaser Orth
Now Major of the
Second Battalion

(Unpublished documents pertaining to Lebanon County — Pge 44)

More could be learned about the military service of Balthaser Orth by reviewing the federal pension files for men who served under him. The list of men in Appendix "Z" has only been partially searched for this information.

CHAPTER 14

JOHN STONE

John Stone was a Captain of the 6th company of the Second Battalion of Lancaster Militia on May 9, 1780 under Lieutenant Colonel Thomas Edwards (Notes and Queries, Series 3, Volume 3, Page 547, W.H. Egle). A partial list of the privates serving under him follows:

John David Braun	February 11, 1763	March 11, 1820
Jacob Dieffenbach	1744	1803
John Adam Garman	December 13, 1754	1823
Philip Lorenz Houtz	September, 1712	October 22, 1788
Abraham Krall	1743	1823
John Conrad Miller	September 28, 1752	November 23, 1823
Jacob Rittel	September 1, 1761	November 21, 1826
Heinrich Rudi	1744	1816
Abraham Schmutz	September 13, 1764	August 23, 1792
Issac Shaffer	January 16, 1760	May 1, 1801
John Wendel Shott	January 17, 1761	April 23, 1833
Jacob Sigs	July 25, 1741	August 23, 1820
Peter Spyker	October 7, 1711	July 8, 1789
Frederick Stager	August 28, 1760	February 18, 1826
Michael Tice	February 2, 1728	March 20, 1804

This list was compiled from a listing of Lebanon County Tombstone inscriptions of revolutionary soldiers. Only one man on this list lived long enough to apply for the 1832 Pension Act, but no pension file could be found.

On January 19, 1781 John Stone sold 10 bushels of rye to the State of Pennsylvania for £2.16.8 and signed a receipt for P. Marsteller. (Some hitherto unpublished documents pertaining to Lebanon County's part in the war of the Revolution, Shenk, H. H., 1916).

In September 1781 Captain John Stone's company is listed as guarding prisoners at Lebanon and Lancaster. (Lebanon County's part in the Revolutionary War, Richards, H.M.M., Page 395).

CHAPTER 15

JOHN MICHAEL SMYSER

John Michael Smyser was the most active and prominent member of his immediate family to serve in the Revolutionary War. As early as 1775 "He was one of a committee of 12 from York County who raised money to send to the inhabitants of Boston, when the port of that city was closed by the British; collecting 6£ 12S.1d. from his own township, which amount was the most raised by any one person". (History of the Smyser Family in America - 1731-1931).

John Michael Smyser was a captain of the first company under Colonel Michael Swope in the Pennsylvania Flying Camp. Michael Copenhaver described service as a private under Captain Smyser in his pension Application S22690 (Appendix "AA"). He said this service was for 6 months starting in July 1776 and that they were stationed near Fort Lee during part of this period. There are two other sources of information which say that Captain Smyser was at Fort Washington at the time of its capture by the British on September 16, 1776, and that he was a prisoner of war for several months. (History of the Smyser Family in America 1731 - 1931, and Lancaster County Connections Volume 1, No. 4, Page 29). An additional source, (The Pennsylvania-German in the Revolutionary War 1775 - 1783, Richards) which refers to this period says, "In July, 1776, five battalions of the York County emergency men were enrolled for duty with Washington. Two of these battalions saw active service. — The first battalion, commanded by Colonel Michael Swope, was almost entirely German. It suffered very severely at Long Island and Fort Washington." Michael Smyser was listed as captain of the first company on the roster.

More information in support of the military service of John Michael Smyser can be found in the pension applications of Adam Wolf, S3615 and George Eisenhart, R3275.

In 1778 John Michael Smyser was elected a member of the House of Representatives of Pennsylvania from York County and was re-elected 7 times. From 1790 to 1795 he represented his county in the state senate, being the first person elected to that office under the state constitution of 1790. (Gibsons History of York County).

At sometime late in his military career John Michael Smyser held the rank of lieutenant colonel of the 3rd Battalion of York County Militia. This information is listed in the D.A.R. Lineage Books, but I cannot determine what time period he served in this capacity.

John Michael Smyser died in 1810 at nearly 70 years of age, but long before he could have qualified for a federal pension for his service.

CHAPTER 16

JACOB MATHIAS SMYSER

Jacob Mathias Smyser was one of the three sons of Mathias Smyser and Anna Catherine Copenhaver who served in the Revolutionary War. He was a private in Captain Emanuel Herman's Company in 1777 in the 2nd Battalion of York County Militia (Prowell's History of York County, Pages 273-275).

As of this writing I have been unable to find any other references to his military service.

CHAPTER 17

MATHIAS EMERICK SMYSER

Mathias Emerich Smyser was the youngest son of Mathias Smyser and Anna Catherine Copenhaver to serve in the Revolutionary War. Unfortunately there are only two secondary sources of information pertaining to his service. The book "History of the Smyser Family in America 1731 - 1931" says that he served as a private in Captain Emanuel Herman's company in 1777 in the 2nd Battalion of York County Militia. There is also mention of his service in Captain Reinhart Boot's Company of York County Militia in the D.A.R. Lineage Book Volume 89, Page 203. Mathias Emerick Smyser died in 1829 just prior to the enactment of the law which would have allowed him a pension for his service. If he would have lived long enough to apply for a pension perhaps we would know more about his activities during the Revolutionary War.

CHAPTER 18

CHRISTIAN WALBORN

From the tombstone of Christian Walborn in Union Cemetery in Myerstown, Pennsylvania we learn that he was in the 3rd Company of the 2nd Battalion of Lancaster County Militia. Unfortunately, no dates can be found. If the service occurred in May of 1780 he was in the company of Captain Casper Stoever. If the service occurred in April of 1783 he was in the company of Captain Jacob Meily. More research is necessary to learn about Christian Walborn's service in the Revolutionary War.

CHAPTER 19

THOMAS COPENHAVER

Thomas Copenhaver was reported to be a drummer boy at the age of 14 in the Revolutionary War (Viola K. Mohn, Personal Communication, 1983). This event presumably occurred in 1776, however, I can find no documentation to support this statement.

From May 1, 1781 to June 30, 1781 Thomas Copenhaver was on the muster roll in Class Two, 2nd Battalion of Lancaster during this period. Thomas Copenhaver hired Martin Jordan to act as his substitute during this two month period. (Pennsylvania Archives, Series 5, Volume 7, Page 126).

In 1782 Thomas Copenhaver was in the 2nd Class of Captain Wendel Weaver's 7th Company of the Second Battalion of Lancaster County Militia. (Pennsylvania Archives, Series 5, Volume 7, Page 181).

On July 10, 1794 Thomas Copenhaver is listed in the fourth class of Captain William Young's company of Pennsylvania Militia, no county designation is given, but it is undoubtedly Lancaster County. (Pennsylvania Archives, Series 6, Volume 5, Page 252).

Thomas Copenhaver died on February 27, 1845 even though he lived 13 years after the Pension Act of 1832 went into effect. I cannot find where he applied for a Federal Pension.

CHAPTER 20

MARTINUS COPENHAVER

Martinus Copenhaver was born on March 7, 1760 and was therefore too young to participate during the early years of the war. Cornelius Koppenheffer says that Martinus was in Captain Henry Nach's Company of Militia in Alsace Township, Berks County, Pennsylvania on January 1, 1784. (Personal Communication 1984). I have found no documentation for this nor any reference to any other service, for Martinus Copenhaver at this time.

CHAPTER 21

JOHAN MICHAEL COPENHAVER

Michael Copenhaver enlisted as a private in the First Battalion of York County Militia on December 27, 1775 under Captain George Eichelberger when he was only 17 years old. A complete listing of this company appears in the Pennsylvania Archives, Series 6, Volume 2, Pages 419-420. From his pension application Appendix "AA" we learn that he joined the company of Captain Yost Garbaugh about July 1, 1776. They marched from Lancaster to Philadelphia, took a boat to Trenton and then marched to Perty Amboy, Bergen and finally to Elizabeth, New Jersey. Michael Copenhaver then joined the Flying Camp for 6 months under Captain Michael Smyser and Colonel Michael Swope. He was "laying sick in the neighborhood of Fort Lee at the time that Colonel Swope was taken prisoner".

The next information we have about his service is from the Pennsylvania Archives 6th Series, Volume 2, Page 655 where Michael Copenhaver is listed as a sergeant under Captain Simon Copenhaver, his father, on February 5, 1782.

Michael was granted a Pennsylvania state pension in 1830 under P.L. 217. More information might be gathered about his military service if he gave any testimony to support his state pension application.

CHAPTER 22

MARTIN COPENHAVER

Martin Copenhaver was a private in the Second Class of a Company of unknown Battalion of York County Militia in February 1782 or 1783. His service was performed under his father, Captain Simon Copenhaver. The roster of this company is listed in Appendix "O". No other reference to Martin Copenhaver's military service has been found.

CHAPTER 23

SIMON COPENHAVER II

Simon Copenhaver II was only about 16 years old when he appeared as a private on the muster roll of the 3rd Company, probably 2nd Battalion, York County Militia in 1772 or 1778. (Appendix "P") His Father Simon Copenhaver was the company commander. By November 1, 1781 he had apparently risen to the rank of sergeant of the same company. (Cornelius Koppenheffer Correspondence, 1984)

In October 1783 Simon Copenhaver II was one of the signers of a petition sent to John Dickinson, ESQ., President of the Supreme Executive Council of the Commonwealth of Pennsylvania, to keep the militia quartered at Yorktown County. Simon was in the army at this time. (PA. Dutchman, CE. Koppenheffer Nov. 15, 1950)

Simon died in 1832 just prior to the time when he could have applied for a federal pension.

CHAPTER 24

MICHAEL BROWN

Michael Brown was a son-in-law of Captain Thomas Copenhaver. On August 12, 1776 he is listed as being a private in the company of Captain Copenhaver in Colonel Timothy Green's battalion (Appendix "A"). It can be presumed that his military service during the fall of 1776 is the same as appears in Chapter 5 for Captain Thomas Copenhaver.

A man named Michael Brown signed an Oath of Allegiance to the patriot cause on May 5, 1778, but I cannot determine if it is the same man who is discussed here.

There is also a Captain Michael Brown, Jr. who commanded the Fourth Company of the First Battalion of Lancaster County Militia on April 15, 1778, but I cannot determine if it is the same man who is discussed here.

There is also a Captain Michael Brown, Jr. who commanded the Fourth Company of the First Battalion of Lancaster County Militia on April 15, 1783. (Pennsylvania German in the Revolutionary War, Richards, H.M.M. Page 374). I cannot determine who is who because Michael Brown is such a common name.

CHAPTER 25

THOMAS COPENHAVER III

Soon after the family of Captain Thomas Copenhaver moved to Montgomery County, Virginia from Pennsylvania in 1780 Thomas Copenhaver III volunteered for a tour of militia duty under Captain William Gleaves in the North Carolina campaign. (Pension Application R2311, National Archives) Appendix "S." This tour of duty is described in court testimony by Thomas Copenhaver in 1834 when he was 70 years old. He was only 17 years old during the time he served 4 tours of militia duty as a volunteer. "William Glaves was my captain. I entered the service in the month of August in the year 1780. Our tour of service was for two months at which time the company was discharged. We was in no engagement during the time I resided in Montgomery County, Virginia when I entered the service, which was as a volunteer, we rendezvoused at the lead mines (Fort Chiswell) in Montgomery County, Virginia. From there we marched into North Carolina to Hoosier Town. When I was taken sick and left behind. We served with no regular troops, having volunteered in a call from the proper authority to go against and keep in subjection the tories who at times had nearly over ran North Carolina. The company I belonged to was engaged in North Carolina where I cannot say as I was left behind sick as before stated. Many of the men came back by the way of Hoosier Town with whom I returned home."

The second tour of militia duty that Thomas Copenhaver served was under Colonel William Preston in late 1780 or early 1781. More is known about this tour of duty not because of what Thomas tells us in his pension application, but because he served with more prominent people and participated in some events that were recorded by several individuals.

On February 8, 1781 General Nathaniel Greene requested the support of various militia units for his forthcoming campaign in the southern department. On February 18th Colonel William Preston responded to this request and said he would march with 300 men from the lead mines at Fort Chiswell to join Lt. Colonel Henry Lee and General Nathaniel Greene in North Carolina. On February 20th Lord Cornwallis issued a proclamation from Hillsborough for the Tories to join his regular troops. On February 25th the battle called Pyles defeat took place when Lt. Colonel Henry Lee and his command ambushed a group of Tories who were responding to Lord Cornwallis's call for support. Soon after Pyles' defeat (possibly even later that day) Colonel William Preston and his command of 300 Montgomery County Mountain militia volunteers joined the camp of General Andrew Pickens and Lt. Colonel Henry Lee. Thomas Copenhaver III was a 17 year old private in the group of men commanded by Colonel William Preston in this camp.

The next day Colonel Preston and Lt. Colonel Lee with their command marched to attack Banastre Tarleton as he crossed the Haw River Ford. This is probably the battle that Thomas Copenhaver referres to in his pension application.

On March 1 Preston, Lee and Pickens were all attached to the command of Colonel Otho Williams. On March 2 the men commanded by Colonel Preston and Lt. Colonel Lee attacked the advance of the British Army under Banastre Tarleton and killed and wounded about 30 of them on Allamance Creek. The patriots suffered 3 killed and 10 wounded. It is hard to determine exactly where Thomas Copenhaver was at the time of these 2 battles although we know that part of Colonel Preston's men were engaged on March 2nd and all of his men were engaged in the March

60

6th action. In the second battle (called the Battle of Wetzell's Mill on Reedy Fork) it is reported that the patriots were broken and dispersed with loss of blankets. After the March 6th battle General Greene ordered all of the militia horses sent home because of the lack of forage. The Montgomery County militia most surely went home soon after March 6th and definitely before the March 15th Battle of Guilford Courthouse.

Thomas Copenhaver was not again active in the patriot cause until 1782 when he served in two militia campaigns against the Indians under Captain Robert Davis.

There has been published stories and oral family tradition that Thomas Copenhaver III participated in the Battle of Kings Mountain. I do not think that this is the case. First, Thomas does not mention it in his pension application. Second, he does not appear in any of the published list of Kings Mountain participants and Colonel William Preston was not at Kings Mountain with his command. Part of the confusion may be because Colonel William Campbell of the Washington County Militia was at Kings Mountain with his command; and Thomas Copenhaver states that he served under a certain Lieutenant William Campbell during October 1780 when the Battle of Kings Mountain took place. Lt. William Campbell and Colonel William Campbell were not the same individual. (See muster roll at Appendix "BB")

CHAPTER 26

JACOB LEHMAN

During the time of the Revolutionary War there were numerous men named Jacob Lehman (and other spellings) living in Lancaster County. It is not possible to tell with certainty who was who. A Jacob Lehman is listed as ensign of Captain John Gassert's 8th Company of the Second Battalion of Lancaster County Militia on May 6, 1780. (Richards, H.M.M., Lebanon County's part in the Revolutionary War, Page 395).

A man named Jacob Lehman served under Captain Thomas Copenhaver in January 1777 along with John Bickel (Appendix "J"). If either of these Jacob Lehmans is the son of Christian Lehman and therefore the nephew of Captain Copenhaver then it is possible to document his military service. I presume that the Jacob Lehman who served under Captain Thomas Copenhaver was his nephew because it was customary for relatives and close neighbors to be in the same unit. The Jacob Lehman from Appendix "J" lived long enough to apply for the 1832 Pension, but, though I have made an exhaustive search I cannot find his pension application which would help us determine exactly who he was.

CHAPTER 27

CHRISTOPHER COPENHAVER, JR.

Christopher Copenhaver, Jr. is listed as a Private in the 2nd Class of Captain Wendel Weaver's Seventh Company of the 2nd Battalion of Lancaster County Militia in 1782. (Pennsylvania Archives, Series 5, Volume 7, Page 181). Christopher was only 19 years old in 1782 and this is probably the first military unit he was associated with. It may be the only military unit he was in.

On May 25, 1778 Christian Copenhaver took the Oath of Allegiance. (Pennsylvania Archives, Series 2, Volume 13, Page 415). Cornelius Koppenheffer thinks that these are the same person. I don't think this is the case. Christopher would have only been 15 years old in 1778 and I don't believe that Christopher and Christian are equivalent given names.

CHAPTER 28

CHRISTIAN LEY

Christian Ley appears twice on the muster rolls of Captain Wendel Weaver's Seventh company in the 2nd Battalion of Lancaster County Militia in both 1781 and 1782. In each case, he is listed in the first class. (Pennsylvania Archives, Series 5, Volume 7, Pages 160 and 180).

On his tombstone in the Union Cemetery in Myerstown, Pennsylvania he is listed as a Sergeant in the 2nd Battalion of Lancaster County Militia. He attained the rank of sergeant and was only 20 years old in 1782. He lived to be 69 years old and died in 1832, but apparently did not apply for a Federal pension.

CHAPTER 29

JOHANNES ORTH

Johannes Orth was born in 1760. He was the son of Adam Orth and Anna Catherine Kucher. He was not active in the early years of the war due to his age, but by May 6, 1780 he had attained the rank of lieutenant in the 1st Company of the Second Battalion of the Lancaster County Militia. He served under his uncle Captain Balthaser Orth and Lt. Colonel Thomas Edwards. (Lebanon County in the Revolutionary War, Page 395).

By April 15, 1783 Johannes Orth had attained the rank of Captain of the 7th Company of the 2nd Battalion of Lancaster County Militia. He served under Major Balthaser Orth, his uncle, and John Gloninger, his brother-in-law. Another brother-in-law, David Krause was Captain of the 1st Company. (Pennsylvania in the Revolutionary War, Volume 1, Page 375)

Johannes Orth died in 1784 and is buried in the Hebron Moravian Cemetery in Lebanon, PA. (Revolutionary War soldiers buried in Lebanon County, Page 67) I have not found any information relating to his cause of death to determine if it was a result of the war.

CHAPTER 30

DAVID KRAUSE

David Krause was born in Lebanon County in 1752; the son of John Krause a Palatinate immigrant. He commanded a company of associators in the Jersey Campaign of 1776, and in the campaign around Philadelphia in 1777, subsequently he was commissary of Colonel Greenawalt's Battalion. (The Pennsylvania German in the Revolutionary War, Richards, H.M.M.).

On October 29, 1777, he was barrack's master at the Hebron church at Lebanon, Pennsylvania guarding Hessian prisoners. (Lebanon County's Part in the Revolutionary War, Richard, H.M.M., 1909).

Captain David Krause commanded the Fourth Company of the Second Battalion of Lancaster County Militia under Lieutenant Colonel Thomas Edwards and Major Valentine Shouffler on May 6, 1780. (Notes and Queries, Series 3, Volume 3, Page 547). The following is a partial list of privates who served in this company:

Johan Philip Beck	February 2, 1727	February 22, 1792
Thomas Clark	December 7, 1746	October 1, 1804
Heinrich Anthony		
Doebler	January 17, 1783	March 17, 1814
Christopher Embich		
Christopher Embich, Jr.		
John Jacob Embich	October 12, 1754	October 19, 1819
Heinrich Gilbert	December, 1748	August, 1815
George Gloninger	June 17, 1754	April 7, 1831

Philip Gloninger	February 12, 1719	December 11, 1796
Anthony Kelker	December 30, 1733	March 12, 1812
Herny Kelker	January 20, 1761	October 11, 1823
Rudolph Kelker	February 2, 1758	May 30, 1801
Michael Krebs	September 17, 1747	November 2, 1803
Leonard Krumbine		
Johannes Lauser	January 18, 1762	June 9, 1813
Conrad Mark	October 17, 1743	December, 1823
Jacob Peiffer	May 16, 1745	June 12, 1824
Bernhard Reinhard	January, 1759	May 1, 1816
Conrad Reinoel	May 1, 1756	December 22, 1832
George Reinoel	July 10, 1752	December 19, 1832
Peter Shindel	February 28, 1732	May 29, 1782
John Stoehr	1735	1805
Freiderich Stoever	September 20, 1759	May 27, 1833
George Freiderich		
Stroh	November 9, 1741	May 20, 1806
John Thorne	June 15, 1739	1804
Christopher Uhler	1745	1805
John Martin Yensel	November 11, 1746	November 4, 1820

(Revolutionary War Soldiers Buried in Lebanon County)

In November and December 1780, David Krause sold supplies to the State of Pennsylvania. The three following receipts are copied from "Some Hitherto Unpublished Documents Pertaining to Lebanon County's Part in the War of the Revolution, Shenk, H.H., 1916".

> The State of Pennsylvania
> To David Krause, Dr.

to 7 ton of flour − − @ 23 £4 Sc 15	£163.06.8
to 70 casks for __ do- @ 20 Dol.	£ 9.15.0
900 cask nails − − − @ 1 Dol.	£ 9.0
	£172.10.8

Received November 19, 1780 of P. Marstellar the above sum of one hundred and seventy-two pounds, ten shillings, and eight pence in full for the above amount.

David Krause

The State of Pennsylvania
     To David Krause, Dr.
  to 5 ton of flour — — @ 23/.4 Sc   £116.13.4
  to 50 casks for   — @ 2/.   5.00.0
  600 cask nails — — — @ 1/.   0.06.0

                                            £121.19.4

Received December 25, 1780 of P. Marsteller the above sum of one hundred and twenty-one pounds, nineteen shillings and four pence in full for the above amount.

David Krause

The State of Pennsylvania
     to David Krause, Dr.
  to 40 Bu. of fall of wheat wt. 50 Sc @ 5/.£10.0.0

Received December 25, 1780 of P. Marsteller the above sum of ten pounds in full for the above amount.

David Krause

From August 20, 1781 to October 20, 1781, Captain David Krause's company was on duty guarding prisoners. This presumably occurred near Lebanon, Pennsylvania. (Lebanon County's Part in the Revolutionary War, Richards, H.M.M.).

David Krause was listed as Captain of the 4th Company of the Second Battalion of Lancaster County Militia under Colonel Thomas Edwards on December 15, 1781 (The Pennsylvania German in the Revolutionary War, Richards, H.M.M.). He apparently served only in this unit after 1780. More information might be obtained by searching for pension applications of men who served with him. Three of the privates listed earlier survived until 1832 when the Pension act went into effect.

David Krause died on December 29, 1820 and was buried in Salem Cemetery. He was later reinterred in Mt. Lebanon Cemetery.

CHAPTER 31

GOTTLIEB ORTH

Gottlieb Orth served as a private under his father Captain Balthaser Orth in the 1st Company, 2nd Battalion of the Lancaster County Militia in May of 1780 or in 1781. He would have only been 16 or 17 years old at the time. No other information can be found about his service in the Revolutionary War.

CHAPTER 32

JOHN GLONINGER

John Gloninger was born on September 19, 1758 and was very active in the Revolutionary War in spite of this young age. In 1776 or 1777, he served 1 month as a private and 6 months as a corporal under Captain Baylor in the Pennsylvania Militia under Colonel Greenawalt. (Affidavits of Andrew Huber and Dilman Daub, Appendix "U" and "V") . He later served in Colonel Klotz's regiment of the Flying Camp. He was engaged in the battles of Staten Island and Trenton. (Appendix "N")

On May 15, 1780 John Gloninger was a Sergeant Major in the 2nd Battalion of the Lancaster County Militia under Lt. Colonel Thomas Edwards. (Notes and Queries, Series 3, Volume 3, Page 546)

On July 8, 1782 he was appointed Sub-lieutenant for Lancaster County by the Supreme Executive Council. (Penn. Archives, Series 5, Volume 7, Page 183. Also affidavits of Valentine Shouffler and Abraham Sebolt, Appendix "S" and "X")

John Gloninger was Lieutenant Colonel of the Second Battalion of Lancaster County Militia. On April 15, 1783 serving under him were Major Baltzer Orth, Captain David Krause and Captain John Orth.

In 1784 he married Catherine Orth, daughter of Adam Orth. He had a long and distinguished career as a public servant, being elected as a justice of the peace, a member of the Pennsylvania Constitutional Convention, a member of the Pennsylvania Legislature, a member of the legislature of the United States. He died in 1836 after applying for a federal pension which his wife ultimately received.

CHAPTER 33

JACOB COPENHAVER

Jacob Copenhaver is included in this book because he was the only Copenhaver I have found who fought in the Revolutionary War who was not descended from Wolfgang Copenhaver. They may have been distantly related, but Jacob is the son of Jacob who is the son of Niclaus of Monchzell, Baden, Germany. (See Genealogy Charts)

There has been speculation by some that there was more than one Jacob who fought in the war and this may be the case, but almost all of the references I have found seem to be for one man and I will call him Jacob 1746 because that is when he was born. His father Jacob 1705 was not in the war and apparently died before 1768. I can find no Jacob in the Wolfgang Copenhaver line that would help us account for the fact that there was a Jacob Copenhaver who saw Revolutionary War service under Captain Lewis Farmer and Colonel Samuel Miles in the Pennsylvania rifle regiment. He apparently enlisted May 8, 1776 and was missing since August 27, 1776 when the Battle of Long Island took place. (Pennsylvania Archives, Series 2, Volume 10, Page 203 and 211)

Jacob 1746 was surely this man in Pennsylvania even though most of the other references for Jacob 1746 are from Virginia. His move from Pennsylvania to Virginia must have been in late 1776 or early 1777.

Feb. 27, 1774 -	Sophia Catharina Copenhaver born at New Holland, Lancaster County, Pennsylvania. She is the older sister of Jacob Copenhaver; he is born 2 years later, presumably in the same place.
1772	A tax list for Earl Township, Lancaster County, Pennsylvania lists Jacob Copenhaver.
May 8, 1776	Jacob Copenhaver is listed in the company of Captain Lewis Farmer and Colonel Samuel Miles regiment missing since the Battle of Long Island, August 27, 1776. (Pennsylvania Archives, Series 2, Volume 10, Page 203, 211)
No Date	Jacob Copenhaver is listed as a Revolutionary soldier from Pennsylvania (Pennsylvania Archives, Series 2, Volume 13, Page 124)
1777 or Before -	Jacob Copenhaver is on a list of Alexander Machir's company in the Strasburg District, Shenandoah County, Virginia. (National Archives REQ. C 2825 ACCT. NO. 21127 Bird Samuels Papers Original Census and Military Records of Old Dunmore Co., Virginia)
Sept. 14, 1777 -	A daughter is born to Jacob Copenhaver and his wife Susannah in Strasburg, Virginia.

Dec. 20, 1777	-	Jacob Copenhaver bought a house lot in Strasburg, Virginia.
July 30, 1778	-	Jacob Copenhaver bought a house lot in Strasburg, Virginia.
Nov. 7, 1780	-	Jacob Copenhaver wrote his will and says he is "called into the army". (Will Book A, Page 431 Woodstock Courthouse, Shenandoah County, Virginia)
August 29, 1782-		The will of Jacob Copenhaver is probated in Shenandoah County, Virginia.

This sequence of events seems to account for Jacob Copenhaver serving in the war from both Pennsylvania and Virginia. Until more evidence turns up I think there was only 1 Jacob.

Of further interest is his death which occurred between Nov. 7, 1780 and August 29, 1782; was it a war related death? He was only 36 years old.

It is appropriate that I end this chapter and this book with a question, because I feel that there is much more to be learned about the military service of the Copenhaver family in the Revolutionary War. Please add to and correct what I have presented.

BIBLIOGRAPHY

Abstracts of the Records of Augusta County, Virginia, Volume 2.

Bickel, John; Revolutionary War Pension Application S22122 National   Archives, Washington, D.C.

Bird, Samuel; Papers, Account No. 21127, National Archives, Req. C.
      2825.

Canfield, Clifford R.; Personal Communication, 1999.

Coppenhaffer, Michael; Revolutionary War Pension Application S-22690, National Archives, Washington, D.C.

Copenhaver, Mildred M.; Personal Communication, 1984.

Draper, Lyman C.; "King's Mountain and its Hereos: History of the Battle of King's Mountain, October 7, 1780 and the Events Which Led to It," 1881.

Egle, William H. Linn, John B. and Montgomery, Thomas L. eds. Pennsylvania Archives 1874-1914, Harrisburg, Pennsylvania.
      Series I, Volume 3.
      Series II, Volume 1.
      Series II, Volume 10
      Series II, Volume 13.

      Series V, Volume 7.
      Series VI, Volume 2

Egle, William H.; "Egle's Notes and Queries", 12 Volumes 1893-1901.

Egle, William H.; "Genealogical Record of the Families of Beatty, Egle, Mueller, Murray, Orth and Thomas", Harrisburg, L.S. Hart, 1886.

Egle, William H.; "History of the Counties of Dauphin and Lebanon in the Commonwealth of Pennsylvania", Everts and Peck, 1883.

Egle, William H.; "Pennsylvania Genealogies, Chiefly Scotch-Irish and German", Harrisburg, Pennsylvania, 1886.

Egle, William H.; "Some Pennsylvania Women during the War of The Revolution", Harrisburg, Pennsylvania, 1898.

Fiske, John; "The American Revolution", The Riverside Press, 1891.

Gerberich, A.H.; "History of the Gerberich Family in America 1631-1925", Harrisburg, Pennsylvania, 1925.

Gibson, John; "Biographical History of York County, Pennsylvania", 1886.

Harkerader, John; Revolutionary War Pension Application S-13323, National Archives, Washington, D.C.

Hedrick, William; Revolutionary War Pension Application R-4355, National Archives, Washington, D.C.

Heitman, Francis B.; "Historical Register of Officers of the Continental Army During the War of the Revolution, April 1775 - December 1783", 1914.

Hetrick, John; Revolutionary War Pension Application R-4843, National Archives, Washington, D.C.

Hoover, John; Revolutionary War Pension Application S-4402, National Archives, Washington, D.C.

Koppenheffer, C.E.; Personal Communication, 1984.

Kopenhaver, Thomas; Revolutionary War Pension Application R-2311, National Archives, Washington, D.C.

Koppenheffer, C.E.; "Revolutionary War Record of Captain Thomas Koppenheffer", unpublished manuscript.

Lee, Henry; "Memoirs of the War in the Southern Department of the United States", University Publishing Co., 1869.

Lossing, Benson J.; "The Pictoral Field-Book of the Revolution", 2 Volumes, 1860.

Metcalf, Frank J.; "List of 164 Person Who Were Paid For Forage. . .", National Genealogical Society Quarterly, Volume XVI, Number 3, Washington, D.C., 1928.

Mohn, Viola K.; Personal Communication, 1983.

National Society of the Sons of the American Revolution, A National Register of the Society Sons of the American Revolution, 2 Volumes, New York: A.H. Kellogg, 1902, Numbers 90102, 90908, 57006, 99223, 100045.

Pennsylvania Historical and Museum Commission Records of the Comptroller General, at the Division of Archives and Manuscripts, Harrisburg, Pennsylvania, Interest Register B.

Pennsylvania Archives, Colonial Records, Volume 10, Harrisburg, 1852.

Pierce, John; Register of the certificates issued by John Pierce, Paymaster General and Commissioner of army accounts for the United States, to officers and soldiers of the Continental Army under the Act of July 4, 1783. 17th Report of the National Society of the Daughters of the American Revolution, 1915.

Preston, William; "The Preston and Virginia Pagers of the Draper Collection of Manuscripts", Volume I, State Historical Society of Wisconsin.

Public Service Claims, Berkley County, Virginia, Certificate Req. C 2825, Number 148.

Richards, Captain H.M.M.; "Lebanon County's Part in the Revolutionary War", Volume 4, Number 12, 1909.

Richards, Henry M.M.; "The Pennsylvania-German in the Revolutionary War 1775-1783", 1907.

Rupp, Israel D.; "History of Lancaster County", Gilbert Hills, Lancaster, Pennsylvania, 1844.

Rupp, Israel D.; "History of Dauphin County", Gilbert Hills, Lancaster, Pennsylvania, 1845.

Rupp, Israel D.; "History of Berks and Lebanon Counties".

Shenk, H.H.; "Some Hitherto Unpublished Documents Pertaining to Lebanon County's Part in the War of the Revolution", The Lebanon County Historical Society, Volume VII, Number 1, 1916.

Smyser, William E.; "An account of the Smeisser (Schmeisser) Family".

United States Census Bureau, Census of Pensioners for Revolutionary and Military Services and Returned under the Act for Taking the Sixth Census in 1840, Washington, D.C., 1841.

White, Katherine K.; "The King's Mountain Men", 1924.

Wilt, Thomas; Revolutionary War Pension Application W-3322, National Archives, Washington, D.C.

Wisconsin State Historical Society, "Calendar of the Tennessee and King's Mountain Papers of the Draper Collection of Manuscripts", 1929.

Wisconsin State Historical Society, "The Preston and Virginia Papers of the Draper Collection of Manuscripts", 1915.

INTRODUCTION TO GENEALOGY SECTION

This book was not originally conceived to be a genealogy book; but out of necessity, to fulfill the intent of the book, the family relationships had to be documented. This genealogy was compiled from many sources. I have checked the information to make it as accurate and reliable as possible. In some instances, I have taken undocumented, second hand information and incorporated it into the genealogy where original documents could not be studied.

Husband 1

Wolfgang Copenhaver
Birth: ca 1685, Rüblingen, Wurttemberg, Germany
Death: 1752, Heidelberg Township, Lancaster County,
    Pennsylvania
Burial: Probably Christ Lutheran Church near
    Meyerstown, Pennsylvania
Places of Residence: Rüblingen, Germany; Lancaster
    County, Pennsylvania
Immigrant to America, September 11, 1732

Wife

Anna Maria Haffner?
Birth: ca 1689, Germany
Burial: Probably Christ Lutheran Church near
    Meyerstown, Pennsylvania
Immigrant to America, September 11, 1732

Children

1 - Johann Thomas
    Birth: ca 1710, Rüblingen, Wurttemberg, Germany
    Marriage: ca 1728
    Spouse: Anna Maria Zinn?
    Death: Before December 31, 1760
    Immigrant to America, September 11, 1728

2 - Johann Michael
    Birth: ca 1711, Rüblingen, Wurttemberg, Germany
    Spouse: Eva Margaret Strecher
    Immigrant to America, September 11, 1732

3 – Anna Barbara
   Birth: April 21, 1712, Rüblingen, Wurttemberg,
     Germany
   Marriage: October 6, 1735, Lebanon County,
     Pennsylvania
   Spouse: Johann Peter Kucker
   Death: After 1777
   Immigrant to America, September 11, 1732

4 – Anna Rosina (Susanna)
   Birth: February 15, 1715, Rüblingen, Wurttemberg,
     Germany
   Marriage: December 18, 1734, Lebanon County,
     Pennsylvania
   Spouse: Christopher Meyer
   Death: April 12, 1778
   Immigrant to America, September 11, 1732

5 – Anna Catherine
   Birth: June 5, 1717, Rüblingen, Wurttemberg,
     Germany
   Marriage: August 2, 1738, Lebanon County,
     Pennsylvania
   Spouse: Matthias Smyser[R]
   Death: February 13, 1763
   Immigrant to America, September 11, 1732

[R] – Served in Revolutionary War

Husband　　　　　　　**1-1**

Johann Thomas Copenhaver
Birth: ca 1710, Rüblingen, Wurttemberg, Germany
Father: Wolfgang Copenhaver. Mother's maiden name:
　　　Anna Maria Haffner?
Marriage: ca 1728
Other wives: Anna Elizabeth Holtzmann, Catherine
　　　Elizabeth Lehman
Death: Before December 31, 1760
Immigrant to America, September 11, 1728

Wife
Anna Maria Zinn?
Birth: ca 1709, Germany
Father: Peter Zinn (?)
Death: 1746

Children
1 –　Henry[R]
　　　Birth: July 7, 1729, Tulpehocken, Lancaster,
　　　　　Pennsylvania
　　　Marriage: ca 1757
　　　Spouse: Christina Rieth
　　　Death:　February 5, 1809, Meyerstown, Lebanon,
　　　　　Pennsylvania
　　　Burial: Friedens Lutheran Cemetery, Meyerstown,
　　　　　Pennsylvania

2 –　Michael[R]
　　　Birth: 1733, Tulpehocken, Lancaster, Pennsylvania
　　　Marriage: ca 1759

Spouse: Eva Maria Batdorf
Death: Before November 5, 1823,

3 - Simon[R]
Birth: 1735
Marriage: Before 1758
Spouse: 1. Maria Elizabeth Batdorf
Death: August 23, 1802
Burial: Lewisberry, York, Pennsylvania

4 - Thomas[R]
Birth: 1739, Heidelberg Township, Pennsylvania
Marriage: Before 1760
Spouse: Catharina Mosser
Death: 1802, Wythe County, Virginia
Burial: Rural Retreat, Wythe, Virginia

5 - Sophia Margaret Regina
Birth: 1740
Marriage: January 3, 1761
Spouse: John Tice (Deiss)[R]
Death: date unknown

6 - Eva Maria Catherine
Birth: 1741, Lancaster County, Pennsylvania
Marriage: August 30, 1763
Spouse: Christian Lehman III[R]
Death: 1822
Burial: Friedens Lutheran Cemetery, Meyerstown, Pennsylvania

7 - Catherine
Birth: 1745, Lancaster County, Pennsylvania
Marriage: date unknown
Spouse: Michael Bollinger
Death: date unknown
Burial: place unknown

Johann Michael Copenhaver
Birth: ca 1711, Rüblingen, Wurttemburg, Germany
Father: Wolfgang Copenhaver
Marriage: date unknown
Death: date unknown, Heidelberg Township,
   Lancaster, Pennsylvania

Wife
Eva Margaret Strecher
Birth: date, place unknown
Father: unknown
Death: date, place unknown

Children
1 - Christopher
   Birth: June 15, 1737, Heidelberg Township,
      Lancaster County, Pennsylvania
   Marriage: date unknown
   Spouse: Anna Barbara Schnebly
   Death: September 1785, place unknown
   Burial: place unknown

2 - Unknown

3 - Michael[R]
   Birth: 1740, Heidelberg Township, Pennsylvania
   Marriage: unknown
   Spouse: unknown
   Death: ca 1785
   Burial: place unknown

4 - Unknown

5 - Barbara
   Birth: 1744?
   Marriage: unknown

Spouse: unknown
Death: unknown
Burial: unknown

6 - Johannes
Birth: October 7, 1744, Heidelberg Township,
Lancaster, Pennsylvania.
Christened October 23, 1744
Marriage: unknown
Spouse: unknown
Death: date unknown
Burial: place unknown

7 - Anna Barbara
Birth: February 30, 1746, Heidelberg Township,
Lancaster, Pennsylvania.
Christened March 9, 1746
Marriage: date unknown
Spouse: Christian Walborn, Jr.
Death: date unknown
Burial: place unknown

Johann Peter Kucher
Birth: May 12, 1710, Waldau, Brandenburg, Germany
Father: George Peter Kucher; mother - Barbara
Marriage: October 6, 1735, Lebanon, Lancaster,
    Pennsylvania
Occupation: farmer, blacksmith
Church affiliation: Lutheran, Moravian
Death: December 24, 1774, Lancaster County,
    Pennsylvania

Wife
Anna Barbara Copenhaver
Birth: April 21, 1712, Rüblingen, Wurttemburg,
    Germany
Father: Wolfgang Copenhaver; mother - Anna Maria
    Zinn?
Death: After 1777
Burial: Hebron Moravian Cemetery, Lebanon County,
    Pennsylvania

Children
1 - Johann Frantz
    Birth: July 13, 1736. Baptized August 1, 1736
    Marriage: unknown
    Spouse: unknown
    Death: 1748
    Burial: Moravian Cemetery, Lancaster County,
        Pennsylvania

2 - Anna Catherine
   Birth: January 12, 1738; baptized February 7, 1738
   Marriage: May 24, 1757
   Spouse: Adam Orth[R]
   Death: September 16, 1794
   Burial: Moravian Cemetery, Lancaster County,
      Pennsylvania

3 - Johann Christopher[R]
   Birth: March 15, 1739, or March 19, 1739; baptized
      April 22, 1739
   Marriage: date unknown
   Spouse: Mary
   Death: date unknown
   Burial: place unknown

4 - Rosina[R]
   Birth: March 19, 1741, or March 20, 1741; baptized
      March 25, 1741
   Marriage: date unknown
   Spouse: Balthaser Orth[R]
   Death: April 3, 1814
   Burial: Moravian Cemetery, Lancaster County,
      Pennsylvania

5 - Johann Peter
   Birth: January 12, 1743, or February 12, 1743;
      baptized March 27, 1743
   Marriage: never married
   Death: 1783
   Burial: Moravian Cemetery, Lancaster County,
      Pennsylvania

6 - Eva Barbara
   Birth: January 19, 1745
   Marriage: February 6, 1766
   Spouse: John Stone (Stein)[R]
   Death: date unknown
   Burial: place unknown

7 - George Michael
   Birth: February 10, 1747
   Death: March 18, 1748
   Burial: Moravian Cemetery, Lancaster County,
   Pennsylvania

8 - Johann Michael
   Birth: 1749
   Death: 1751
   Burial: Moravian Cemetery, Lancaster County,
   Pennsylvania

9 - Gottleib
   Birth: April 8, 1753
   Marriage: never married
   Death: October 3, 1776
   Burial: Moravian Cemetery, Lancaster County,
   Pennsylvania

10 - Elizabeth
   Birth: 1755
   Death: 1755
   Burial: Moravian Cemetery, Lancaster County,
   Pennsylvania

Husband 1-4

Christopher Meyer
Birth: unknown
His father: unknown
Marriage: December 18, 1734, Lebanon, Lancaster,
    Pennsylvania
Death: date unknown

Wife

Anna Rosina Susanna Copenhaver
Birth: February 15, 1715, Rüblingen, Wurttemburg,
    Germany
Father: Wolfgang Copenhaver; mother – Anne Maria
    Zinn?
Death: April 12, 1778

Children

1 - John George
    Birth: December 4, 1735. Christened April 1736
    Marriage: unknown
    Spouse: unknown
    Death: date unknown
    Burial: place unknown

2 - Maria Barbara
    Birth: August 12, 1738 (?). Christened May 21, 1738
    (?)
    Marriage: unknown
    Spouse: unknown
    Death: date unknown
    Burial: place unknown

3 - Anna Maria
    Birth: June 16, 1742. Christened July 1742
    Marriage: unknown
    Spouse: unknown
    Death: date unknown
    Burial: place unknown

Matthias Smyser[R]
Birth: February 15, 1715, Rügelbach, Wurttemburg,
     Germany. Christened February 17, 1715
Father: Martin Smyser; mother – Anna Barbara Kalther
Marriage: August 2, 1738, North Annville, Lancaster,
     Pennsylvania
Death: April 12, 1778
Burial: First Lutheran Church, York County,
     Pennsylvania

Wife
Anna Catherine Copenhaver
Birth: June 5, 1717, Rüblingen, Wurttemburg, Germany
Father: Wolfgang Copenhaver; mother – Anna Maria
     Zinn?
Death: February 13, 1763, York County, Pennsylvania
Burial: First Lutheran Church, York County,
     Pennsylvania

Children
1 - John George
     Birth: December 23, 1739, York County,
          Pennsylvania
     Marriage: 1760, Christ Lutheran Church
     Spouse: (first name unknown) Mulhaus
     Death: before 1763
     Burial: place unknown

2 - John Michael[R]
Birth: November 21, 1740, York County,
Pennsylvania
Marriage: date unknown
Spouse: Anna Maria Hoke
Death: July 7, 1810
Burial: place unknown

3 - Jacob Mathias[R]
Birth: October 3, 1742, York County, Pennsylvania
Marriage: ca 1766
Spouse: Elizabeth Eichelberger
Death: 1794 or (1793)
Burial: place unknown

4 - Mathias Emerick[R]
Birth: November 1, 1744, York County,
Pennsylvania
Marriage: March 5, 1770
Spouse: Louisa Slagle
Death: February 21, 1829
Burial: place unknown

5 - Maria Dorothea
Birth: March 19, 1747, York County, Pennsylvania
Marriage: date unknown
Spouse: Peter Hoke
Death: January 10, 1815
Burial: place unknown

6 - Rosanna (Rosina)
Birth: February 2 or (12), 1749, York County,
Pennsylvania
Marriage: date unknown
Spouse: George Maul (Moul)
Death: 1796/7
Burial: place unknown

7 - Mary Sabina
Birth: December 14, 1750, York County,
Pennsylvania
Marriage: date unknown
Spouse: John Jacob Swope
Death: date unknown
Burial: place unknown

8 - Elizabeth
Birth: March 21, 1753, York County, Pennsylvania
Marriage: date unknown
Spouse: Leonard Eichelberger
Death: date unknown
Burial: place unknown

9 - Anna Maria
Birth: 1757, York County, Pennsylvania.
Christened May 29, 1757
Marriage: date unknown
Spouse: Martin Ebert
Death: 1833
Burial: place unknown

10 - Susana
Birth: date unknown, York County, Pennsylvania.
Baptized June 26, 1760
Marriage: date unknown
Spouse: Philip Ebert
Death: 1840
Burial: place unknown

11 - Henry
No other information available

Husband 1-1-1

Henry Copenhaver[R]
Birth: July 7, 1729, Tulpehocken, Lancaster County,
    Pennsylvania
Father: Johann Thomas Copenhaver; mother – Anna
    Maria Zinn?
Marriage: ca 1757
Death: February 5, 1809, Myerstown, Lebanon County,
    Pennsylvania
Burial: Friedens Lutheran Cemetery, Myerstown
    County, Pennsylvania

Wife
Christina Rieth
Birth: June 11, 1737, Womelsdorf, Berks County,
    Pennsylvania
Father: J. Michael Rieth; mother – Maria Barbara Faeg
    (Faig)
Death: March 3, 1815
Burial: Friedens Lutheran Cemetery, Myerstown
    County, Pennsylvania

Children
1 - Elizabeth
    Birth: March 16, 1758
    Marriage: February 29, 1780
    Spouse: Christopher Breidenbach
    Death: date unknown
    Burial: place unknown

2 - Catherina
    Birth: February 21, 1760. Christened March 16,
        1760
    Marriage: December 9, 1783
    Spouse: Christian Walborn[R]
    Death: June 9, 1855
    Burial: place unknown

3 - Thomas[R]
    Birth: January 31, 1762, Tulpehocken, Berks
        County, Pennsylvania. Christened February 24,
        1762
    Marriage: date unknown
    Spouse: Catharina Eckert
    Death: February 27, 1845
    Burial: place unknown

4 - Eva
    Birth: July 9, 1763. Christened July 31, 1763
    Marriage: April 20, 1786
    Spouse: Friederick Siebert
    Death: date unknown
    Burial: place unknown

5 - Daniel
    Birth: April 2, 1765. Christened May 5, 1765
    Marriage: unknown
    Spouse: unknown
    Death: date unknown
    Burial: place unknown

6 - Anna Margaret
    Birth: August 29, 1766
    Marriage: date unknown
    Spouse: Martin Walborn
    Death: September 10, 1834
    Burial: place unknown

7 - Maria Barbara
    Birth: July 12, 1769. Christened July 30, 1769
    Marriage: December 9, 1789
    Spouse: David Kilmer
    Death: date unknown
    Burial: place unknown

8 - Anna Christina
   Birth: March 21, 1772. Christened April 19, 1772
   Marriage: February 21, 1798
   Spouse: Phillip Henry Houtz
   Death: date unknown
   Burial: place unknown

9 - Maria Margaretha
   Birth: May 25, 1774. Christened June 14, 1774
   Marriage: December 11, 1811
   Spouse: Daniel Killmer
   Death: date unknown
   Burial: place unknown

10 - Johannes
   Birth: December 6, 1775. Christened January 2,
      1776
   Marriage: date unknown
   Spouse: Margaret Eva _____
   Death: date unknown
   Burial: place unknown

11 - Henry
   Birth: June 19, 1778, Tulpehocken, Berks County,
      Pennsylvania. Christened July 23, 1778
   Marriage: January 16, 1802
   Spouse: Maria Barbara Haak
   Death: August 13, 1823
   Burial: place unknown

12 - Christina
   Birth: November 18, 1780
   Marriage: unknown
   Spouse: unknown
   Death: date unknown
   Burial: place unknown

Husband   **1-1-2**
Michael Copenhaver[R]
Birth: 1733, Tulpehocken, Lancaster County,
      Pennsylvania
Father: Thomas Copenhaver; mother: Anna Maria
      Zinn?
Marriage: ca 1759
Death: before November 5, 1823, Bethel Township,
      Lancaster County, Pennsylvania

Wife
Eva Maria Batdorf
Birth: date unknown
Father: Johannes Martin Batdorf; mother: Maria
      Elizabeth Walborn
Death: date unknown

1 - Martinus[R]
    Birth: March 7, 1760. Christened March 23, 1760
    Marriage: May 2, 1786
    Spouse: Susanna Artz
    Death: January 18, 1825
    Burial: place unknown

2 - Maria Elizabeth
    Birth: May 1, 1763. Christened May 29, 1763
    Marriage: date unknown
    Spouse: William Bordner
    Death: date unknown
    Burial: place unknown

3 - Johannes
    Birth: August 28, 1765. Christened October 13, 1765
    Marriage: June 2, 1789
    Spouse: Margaretha Zerbe
    Death: date unknown
    Burial: place unknown

4 - Maria Catherine
Birth: November 17, 1766/7.
Christened December 25, 1766/7
Marriage: Before 1799
Spouse: George Bonawitz
Death: ca 1812
Burial: place unknown

5 - Michael
Birth: October 5, 1772, Rehrersburg, Berks County,
Pennsylvania. Christened October 18, 1772
Marriage: December 13, 1797, Christ Lutheran
Church, Tulpehocken
Spouse: Catharine Geret (Garrett)
Death: March 7, 1844
Burial: St. John's Lutheran Church, Berrysburg,
Mifflin Township, Pennsylvania

6 - Frederick
Birth: June 21, 1776
Marriage: date unknown
Spouse: Maria Elizabeth Gross
Death: date unknown
Burial: place unknown

7 - Eva Christina?
Birth: date unknown
Marriage: March 29, 1796
Spouse: Johannes Jacob Moyer
Death: date unknown
Burial: place unknown

8 - Eva Margaretta?
Birth: December 2, 1768. Christened December 25,
1768
Marriage: unknown
Spouse: unknown
Death: date unknown
Burial: place unknown

9 - Anna Catharine?
   Birth: July 17, 1771
   Marriage: unknown
   Spouse: unknown
   Death: date unknown
   Burial: place unknown

Husband   **1-1-3**
Simon Copenhaver[R]
Birth: 1735
Marriage: Before 1758
Death: August 23, 1802, Lewisberry, York,
      Pennsylvania
Burial: Bats Nest Cemetery, Lewisberry
Father: Johan Thomas Copenhaver; mother: Anna
      Maria Zinn?

Wife
Maria Elizabeth Batdorf
Birth: February 12 or 13, 1737
Death: ca 1785
Father: Johannes Martin Batdorf; mother: Maria
      Elizabeth Walborn

Children
1 - Simon
      Birth: February 13, 1758, Tulpehocken, Berks
      County, Pennsylvania
      Death: Probably before November 15, 1762

2 - Johann Michael[R]
      Birth: October 15, 1759, Heidelberg Township,
      Lancaster County, Pennsylvania
      Spouse: Jane Gutwalt
      Death: July 28, 1836

3 - Martin[R]
      Birth: January 25, 1761, Tulpehocken, Berks
      County, Pennsylvania
      Spouse: Anna Mary Wentz
      Death: March 4, 1824

4 - Simon[R]
Birth: November 15, 1762
Spouse: Anna Elizabeth Wolfe
Death: August 13, 1832

5 - Eva Maria Elizabeth
Birth: January 17, 1763, Tulpehocken, Berks
County, Pennsylvania
Spouse: John Sands
Death: date unknown

6 - Johann
Birth: November 25, 1764
Spouse: unknown
Death: date unknown

7 - Anna Margaret (?)
Christened: September 19, 1766
Spouse: unknown
Death: date unknown

8 - Benjamin
Birth: September 30, 1766, Tulpehocken, Berks
County, Pennsylvania
Spouse: unknown
Death: date unknown

9 - Maria Barbara
Birth: December 19, 1770, Tulpehocken, Berks
County, Pennsylvania
Spouse: George W. Davits
Death: date unknown

10 - Maria Elizabeth
    Christened: July 31, 1772, York, Pennsylvania
    Spouse: unknown
    Death: date unknown

11 - Catherina
    Birth: date unknown
    Spouse: Abraham Rankin
    Death: date unknown

Husband   **1-1-4**
Thomas Copenhaver[R]
Birth: 1739, Heidelberg Township, Lancaster County,
    Pennsylvania
Marriage: Before 1760
Death: 1802, Wythe County, Virginia
Burial: Rural Retreat, Wythe County, Virginia
    (probably St. Pauls Evangelical Church
    Cemetery
Father: Johan Thomas Copenhaver; mother: Anna
    Maria Zinn?

Wife
Catherina Mosser
Birth: date unknown
Death: Before 1778
Father: John Jacob Mosser; mother: Maria Hostettler?

Children
1- Maria Catherine
    Birth: July 8. 1760, Hanover Township, Lancaster
        County, Pennsylvania
    Marriage: June 24, 1777, Hanover Township,
        Lancaster County, Pennsylvania
    Spouse: Michael Moyers
    Death: date unknown

2 - Christianna
    Birth: date unknown
    Marriage: date unknown
    Spouse: Michael Brown (Braun)[R]
    Death: date unknown

3 - Thomas[R]
   Birth: July 16, 1763
   Marriage: date unknown
   Spouse: Barbara Staley
   Death: Before September 26, 1838, in Missouri

4 - Catharine
   Birth: 1765
   Marriage: date unknown
   Spouse: John Rosenbaum
   Death: November 27, 1830

5 - Elizabeth
   Birth: date unknown
   First marriage: February 27, 1793, Wythe County,
      Virginia
   Spouse: Henry Groseclose
   Second marriage: February 17, 1795
   Spouse: Phillip Wiseman
   Death: date unknown

6 - Mary
   Birth: Date unknown
   Marriage: February 29, 1796, Wythe County,
      Virginia
   Spouse: John Wiseman
   Death: date unknown

7 - Frederick
   Birth: January 1, 1770, Hanover Township,
      Lancaster County, Pennsylvania
   Marriage: 1789, Wythe County, Virginia
   Spouse: Eve Phillipi

Death: January 30, 1836, Smyth County, Virginia
Burial: Chilhowie, Smyth County, Virginia

8 - John Paul
    Birth: date unknown
    Marriage: May 4, 1800
    Spouse: Hannah Barrier
    Death: February 17, 1836, Jackson County,
        Alabama
    Burial: Jackson County, Alabama

Second marriage
Wife
Elizabeth M. Miess
Birth: date unknown
Father: John Miess
Marriage: October 27, 1778
Death: ca 1783

Children
1 - Henry
    Birth: ca 1781, Virginia
    Marriage: June 8, 1802
    Spouse: Barbara Vaught
    Death: date unknown, Washington County,
        Virginia

2 - Samuel
    Birth: February 21, 1783, Virginia
    Marriage: February 4, 1802, Pulaski County,
        Kentucky
    Spouse: Levinia Williams

Death: 1846
Burial: Kentucky

Third marriage
Wife
Juliana Six (Seek) (Sieg)
Birth: date unknown
Marriage: before April 13, 1784, Hanover Township,
      Lancaster County, Pennsylvania
Death: 1813

Children
1 - Magdalena (Molly)
      Birth: 1784, Virginia
      Marriage: September 2, 1802, Wythe County,
          Virginia
      Spouse: George Wiseman
      Death: date unknown

Husband   1-1-5
John Tice[R]
Birth: date unknown
Father: Matthias Tice
Marriage: date unknown, Lebanon, Pennsylvania
Death: date unknown

Wife
Sophia Margaretha Regina Copenhaver
Birth: 1740, Lebanon, Pennsylvania
Father: Johann Thomas Copenhaver
Mother: Anna Maria Zinn?
No known children
Death: January 3, 1781

Husband   **1-1-6**
Christian Lehman III[R]
Birth: July 29, 1744
Father: Christian Lehman Jr.; mother: Eva ?
Marriage: August 3 (30?), 1763
Death: June 22, 1819

Wife
Eva Maria Catherina Copenhaver
Birth: 1741, Lebanon County, Pennsylvania
Father: Johan Thomas Copenhaver; mother Anna Maria
    Zinn?
Death: 1822
Burial: Friedens Lutheran Church, Myerstown,
    Pennsylvania

Children
1 - Michael
    Spouse: unknown

2 - Catharina
    Spouse: George Walborn

3 - Benjamin
    Spouse: unknown

4 - Jacob[R]
    Spouse: unknown

5 - Maria
    Spouse: Nicholas Ekert

6 - Daniel
    Spouse: unknown

7 - Sarah
    Spouse: unknown

8 - Lydia

Spouse: first name unknown, surname Siever

9 - Elizabeth
Spouse: Jacob Kuntz

10 - Eve
Spouse: Peter Ginder

11 - Johannes
Spouse: unknown

12 - Tobias (?)
Spouse: unknown

Husband   **1-2-1**
Christopher Copenhaver[R]
Birth: June 15, 1737, Heidelberg Township, Lancaster
    County, Pennsylvania
Father: Michael Copenhaver; mother: Eva Margaret
    Strecher
Marriage: date unknown
Death: September 1785, Heidelberg Township, Lebanon
    County, Pennsylvania
Burial: Friedens Lutheran Church, Myerstown,
    Pennsylvania

Wife
Anna Barbara Schnebly
Birth: November 11, 1745
Father: Leonard Schnebly
Death: December 27, 1817
Burial: Friedens Lutheran Church, Myerstown,
    Pennsylvania

1 - Christopher[R]
    Birth: April 26, 1763
    Spouse: unknown
    Death: 1783 ?

2 - Barbara
    Birth: 1765
    Marriage: May 9, 1784
    Spouse: Michael Tice, Jr.
    Death: date unknown

3 - Anna Catharine
    Birth: July 28, 1769, Lancaster County,
        Pennsylvania
    Marriage: December 19, 1786
    Spouse: Christian Ley[R]
    Death: January 11, 1822
    Burial: Union Cemetery, Myerstown, Pennsylvania

Husband   **1-2-3?**
John Michael Copenhaver[R]
Birth: October 7, 1744, or 1740, Lebanon, Pennsylvania
Father: Johan Michael Copenhaver; mother: Eva
    Margaret Strecher
Marriage: April 3, 1774
Death: date unknown, Baltimore, Maryland
Burial: Green Mountain Cemetery

Wife
Elizabeth Wentz
Birth: 1744?
Second husband: Andreas Albrecht. Marriage: July 9,
    1798
Death: date unknown

Children
1 - John Michael Jr.
    Birth: August 21, 1775, York, York County,
        Pennsylvania
    Spouse: unknown
    Death: date unknown

2 - John
    Birth: February 2, 1777, York County, Pennsylvania
    Spouse: unknown
    Death: date unknown

3 - Maria Elizabeth
    Birth: August 16, 1778
    Spouse: unknown
    Death: date unknown

4 - John Peter

5 - John Jacob

6 - William

7 - Daniel

8 - Maria Barbara

There is confusion about the identify of John Michael Copenhaver 1-2-3. Information has been found for 2 individuals born about the same time (1740) with different wives and different children. At this time, I cannot determine which is the son of Johann Michael Copenhaver Sr. or if it is the same man with 2 different wives (the birthdates of the children do not appear to conflict).

Husband   **1-2-3 ?**
John Michael Copenhaver[R]
Birth: 1740
Father: Johan Michael Copenhaver
Mother: Eva Margaret Strecher
Death: 1785

Wife
Anna Catherine
Birth: 1744 or 1748

Children
1 - Henry

2 - Eva Margaret
     Birth: December 2, 1768

3 - Anna Catharina
     Birth: July 17, 1771

4 - Mary

Husband 1-3-2
Adam Orth[R]
Birth: March 9, 1733, Lebanon County, Pennsylvania
Marriage: May 24, 1757
Death: November 15, 1794, Lebanon County,
    Pennsylvania
Burial: Hebron Church, Lebanon, Pennsylvania

Wife
Anna Catherina Kucher
Birth: January 12, 1738
Father: Peter Kucher
Mother: Anna Barbara Copenhaver
Death: September 17, 1794
Burial: Hebron Church, Lebanon County, Pennsylvania

Children
1 - Elizabeth
    Birth: June 3, 1758
    Death: 1764

2 - Johannes[R]
    Birth: March 9, 1760
    Spouse: unknown
    Death: July 9, 1784

3 - Rosina
    Birth: March 19, 1762
    Spouse: first name unknown, surname Smith
    Death: date unknown

4 - Joseph
Birth: April 3, 1764
Death: January 29, 1796

5 - Maria Elizabeth
Birth: April 5, 1766
Spouses: John Keller; No. 2, ___ Shaffner
Death: date unknown

6 - Catherine
Birth: October 31, 1767, Lebanon County,
Pennsylvania
Spouse: John Gloninger[R]
Death: Date unknown

7 - Regina
Birth: October 9, 1770
Spouse: David Krause[R]
Death: date unknown

8 - Christian Henry
Birth: March 24, 1773
Spouse: Rebecca Rahm
Death: date unknown

9 - Johanna
Birth: January 25, 1777
Spouse: unknown
Death: date unknown

Husband   **1-3-4**

Balthaser Orth[R]
Birth: June 14, 1736, Lebanon Township, Lebanon
    County, Pennsylvania
Marriage: April 26, 1763, Hebron Church, Lebanon
    Township, Pennsylvania
Death: October 20, 1788, or October 6, 1794, Lebanon
    Township, Pennsylvania
Burial: Hebron Church, Lebanon County, Pennsylvania

Wife

Rosina Kucher[R]
Birth: March 19, 1741
Father: Peter Kucher; mother: Anna Barbara
    Copenhaver
Death: April 3, 1814
Burial: Hebron Church, Lebanon Township,
    Pennsylvania

Children

1 - Gottlieb[R]
    Birth: February 23, 1764
    Spouse: Sarah Steiner
    Death: 1831

2 - Andreas
    Birth: February 11, 1765
    Spouse: unknown
    Death: October 16, 1788

3 - Maria Barbara
    Birth: November 9, 1768
    Spouses: Matthias Morrett; No. 2, Martin Light
    Death: May 4, 1851

4 - Johann Jacob
   Birth: October 11, 1766
   Spouse: unknown
   Death: November 6, 1790

5 - Joseph
   Birth: December 19, 1770
   Spouse: Elizabeth Geisman (or Geiserman)
   Death: April 18, 1848

6 - Justina Elizabeth
   Birth: March 3, 1773
   Death: December 2, 1775

7 - Christina Julianna
   Birth: April 22, 1775
   Spouse: unknown
   Death: date unknown

8 - Johanna Catherine
   Birth: December 21, 1777
   Marriage: October 8, 1797
   Spouse: Jacob Widener
   Death: date unknown

Husband   **1-3-6**
John Stone[R]
Birth: date unknown
Marriage: date unknown
Death: date unknown

Wife
Eve Barbara Kucher
Birth: January 19, 1745
Death: date unknown
Father: Peter Kucher; mother: Anna Barbara
     Copenhaver

Children
1 - Joseph
     Birth: date unknown
     Spouse: unknown
     Death: date unknown

2 - Margaret
     Birth: date unknown
     Spouse: unknown
     Death: date unknown

Husband　　　　　　**1-1-1-3**
Thomas Copenhaver[R]
Birth: January 31, 1761
Father: Henry Copenhaver; mother: Christina Rieth
Marriage: date unknown
Death: February 27, 1845
Burial: Reformed Church, Jonestown, Pennsylvania

Wife
Catharina Eckert
Birth: April 10, 1768
Death: November 2, 1837
Burial: Jonestown, Lebanon County, Pennsylvania

Children
1 - Elizabeth
　　　Birth: date unknown
　　　Spouse: Peter Beshore
　　　Death: date unknown

Husband   **1-1-2-1**
Martinus Copenhaver[R]
Birth: March 7, 1760
Father: Michael Copenhaver
Mother: Eva Maria Batdorf
Marriage: May 2, 1786
Death: January 18, 1825

Wife
Susanna Artz
Birth: date unknown
Death: date unknown

Children
1 - Elisabeth
Birth: September 6, 1787, Rehrersburg, Berks
County, Pennsylvania
Marriage: September 20, 1812
Spouse: Johannes Mayer
Death: June 2, 1826

2 - Information unavailable

3 - Eva Maria
Birth: May 26, 1792, Erdman, Dauphin County,
Pennsylvania
Spouse: unknown
Death: date unknown

4 - Information unavailable

5 - Susanna
Birth: September 29, 1799, Erdman, Dauphin
County, Pennsylvania
Spouse: unknown
Death: date unknown

Husband   **1-1-3-2**

John Michael Copenhaver[R]

Birth: October 15, 1758 or 1759, Heidelberg Township, Lancaster County, Pennsylvania

Father: Simon Copenhaver; mother: Maria Elizabeth Batdorf

Marriage: date unknown

Death: July 28, 1836, York County, Pennsylvania

Burial: Quickels Church, Conewago Township, York County, Pennsylvania

Wife

Jane Gutwalt

Birth: date unknown

Death: date unknown, York County, Pennsylvania

Burial: Quickels Church, Conewago Township, York County, Pennsylvania

Children

1 - John Michael
   Birth: date unknown
   Spouse: unknown
   Death: date unknown

2 - Jacob
   Birth: date unknown
   Spouse: unknown
   Death: date unknown

3 - Henry
   Birth: date unknown
   Spouse: unknown
   Death: date unknown

4 - Martin
   Birth: 1792
   Death: 1864

5 - Catherine
   Birth: date unknown
   Spouse: James Rankin or Jonas Hoffman
   Death: date unknown

6 - Elizabeth
   Birth: date unknown
   Spouse: Jacob Wentz
   Death: date unknown

Husband   1-1-3-4
Simon Copenhaver[R]
Birth: November 15, 1762, Tulpehocken, Berks County,
    Pennsylvania
Marriage: date unknown
Death: August 13, 1832
Father: Simon Copenhaver
Mother: Eva Maria Elizabeth Batdorf

Wife
Anna Elizabeth Wolff
Birth: Date unknown
Death: date unknown

Children
1 - Anna Maria
    Christened: April 11, 1784
    Spouse: unknown
    Death: date unknown

2 - Information unavailable

3 - Anna Eva
    Christened: May 11, 1788
    Spouse: unknown
    Death: date unknown

4 - Information unavailable

5 - Magdalena
    Christened: June 15, 1791, York, York County,
    Pennsylvania
    Spouse: unknown
    Death: date unknown

6 - Information unavailable

7 - Simon
   Christened: June 18, 1797, York, York County,
      Pennsylvania
   Spouse: unknown
   Death: date unknown

Husband   **A1**
Niclaus Koppenhoffer
Birth: Date unknown
Marriage: Date unknown
Death: 1736

Wife
Anna Margretha (maiden name unknown)
Birth: date unknown
Death: date unknown

Children
1 - Maria Magdalena
    Birth: January 1, 1704
    Spouse: unknown
    Death: date unknown

2 - Jacob Koppenhoffer
    Birth: November 27, 1705, Mönchzell, Baden,
       Germany
    Marriage: July 3, 1736
    Spouse: Elisabeth Weider
    Death: Date unknown

Husband   **A1-2**
Jacob Koppenhoffer
Birth: November 27, 1705, Mönchzell, Baden, Germany
Father: Niclaus Koppenoffer
Mother: Anna Margaretha ⸺
Marriage: July 3, 1736
Death: before 1768
Immigrant to America, September 11, 1738

Wife
Elisabeth Catharinen Weider
Birth: date unknown
Father: Hans Weider
Death: after 1768

Children
1 - Friedrich Ludwig
    Birth: March 31, 1737, Mönchzell, Baden, Germany
    Spouse: unknown
    Death: date unknown

2 - Johan Balthaser
    Birth: January 1741, New Holland, Lancaster
       County, Pennsylvania
    Spouse: Elisabeth
    Death: Date unknown

3 - Johannes
    Birth: September 2, 1742, New Holland, Lancaster
       County, Pennsylvania
    Spouse: Mary
    Death: date unknown

4 - Sophia Catharina
    Birth: February 27, 1744, New Holland, Lancaster
       County, Pennsylvania
    Married : February 19, 1760
    Spouse: Johannes Diefenbach
    Death: date unknown

5 - Johan Jacob[R]
Birth: June 25, 1746
Spouse: Susannah (Juliana?)
Living in Strasburg, Virginia, in 1777
Death: between 1780-1782, Maryland

6 - Scharlotta
Birth: January 23, 1748, New Holland, Lancaster
County, Pennsylvania
Spouse: unknown
Death: date unknown

7 - Scharlotta
Birth: February 2, 1749
Spouse: unknown
Death: date unknown

MUSTER ROLL OF
CAPTAIN THOMAS KOPPENHEFFER'S COMPANY

COLONEL TIMOTHY GREEN'S BATTALION

Colonel
Timothy Green

Lieutenant-Colonel
Peter Hedrick

Majors
First-John Rogers   Second-Abraham Latcha

Standard Bearer
Richard Crawford

Surgeon
Dr. John Leidig (Lidig)

Captain Thomas Koppenheffer's Company

A muster-roll of Captain Thomas Koppenheffer's company
of militia, Colonel Timothy Green's battalion of Lancaster
County, on their march for the camp in the Jersey's, mustered
in Lancaster, August 12, 1776.

Captain
Thomas Koppenheffer

First Lieutenant
Peter Brightbill (Bridebill)

Second Lieutenant
John Harckenrider (Harkerider)

Sergeants
John Fierabend   George Beasore

Drummer
John Dubbs

Fifer
William Hedrick

Privates

Martin Albright (Albrecht)   John Huber (Hoover)
Matthias Baker   Alexander Kidd
Adam Baumgartner   John McBride
Baltzer Baumgartner   Michael Maurer
John Baumgartner   Henry Merk (Mark)
George Bomberger   John Miller
Peter Brightbill Jr.   Jacob Musser
Michael Brown   Nicholas Poop (Boob)
Nicholas Bruner (Brunner)   Nicholas Poor (Boor)
Jacob Clement (Claman)   Henry Shell (Schell)
Michael Feltin   Nicholas Snider
Jacob Felton   William Snider
Christian Fox   Christian Stuckey
John Fox   Adam Titler
Christopher Frank   Adam Weantling
George Frank   Daniel Weaver
Adam Henig   John Weaver
Fredrick Henig   Jacob Weaver

35 Privates, 50 Shillings each	£87.10.0
2 Sergeants, 50 Shillings each	5.00.0
1 Drummer	2.10.0
1 Fifer	<u>2.10.0</u>
Advance money paid	£97.10.0

Mustered and passed before the committee of observation and inspection in Lancaster the 12th day of August 1776. And the £97.10.0 advance money paid to Captain Thomas Koppenheffer as P. this receipt.

Test. Willi Atlee, Chairman of Committee and their treasurer and paymaster.

Deserter's from Captain Koppenheffer's Co'y

Adam Baumgartner
Baltzer Baumgartner
John Dubbs
Jacob Musser
Adam Titler
They live in Hunnover (Hanover) Township near Adam Harper's.

Pennsylvania Archives Series 5, Volume 7, Pages 1054, 1055.

Pennsylvania Archives Series 2, Volume 13, Pages 305, 318, 319.

APPENDIX "B"

MUSTER ROLL OF
CAPTAIN THOMAS KOPPENHEFFER'S COMPANY

In Colonel Timothy Green's Hanover Rifle Battalion in 1775 and 1776 was the company of Captain Thomas Koppenheffer, which was wholly composed of Lebanon County men.

Roll of Captain Koppenheffer's Company

Captain
Thomas Koppenheffer

First Lieutenants
Peter Brightbeel (Brightbill)
Balser Bumgarner (Baumgartner)

Second Lieutenants
Jacob Tibbins   John Weaver

Non-Commissioned Officers and Privates

Francis Alberdale   Adam Mark
Frederick Beesor (Bashere)   Henry Mark
Henry Bessor (Bashere)   Mertain Milely
                                    (Miley)
Jacob Bessor (Bashere)   Jacob Musser
John Brightbill   Peter Musser
Peter Brightbeel Sr.   Michael Philipy
 (Brightbill)
Peter Brightbeel Jr   John Pickle (Bickle)
(Brightbill)
Adam Bumgarner   Martain Poor
(Baumgartner)

John Bumgarner
(Baumgartner)
Andrew Carvary

George Chidavite
Jacob Clement (Claman)
Nicholas Earhart
(Bruner)
Peter Felty
Adam Fittler (Fidler)
John Fox

Peter Fox
Christopher Frank
George Frank
Phillip Frank
Thomas Frederick
Jacob Gathel
Adam Goodman (Gutman)
John Harper
George Hederick
(Weantling)
William Hederick
Conrad Helm
Henry Hess
(Winder)
Andrew Kaver
Henry Lowmiller
(Laudermilch)
Philip Lydsatricker
John Lymon (Lehman)
John McBride

Nicholas Poor

Nicholas Pupp (Poop)
(Boob)

John Pruner (Bruner)
Nicholas Pruner

Henry Shell (Schell)
Nicholas Snider
Christophel Stoakey
(Stuckey)

Balsor Stone
Michael Straw
George Tittle
Adam Tittler
John Toops (Dupps)
John Walmer
Peter Walmer
Adam Wentling

George Wilt
Jacob Winter

John Winter
John Winter Sr.

History of the counties of Dauphin and Lebanon by William
Henry Egle, 1883, Pages 32, 33.

APPENDIX "C"

ADDITIONAL MEN WHO
SERVED WITH CAPTAIN THOMAS COPENHAVER

John Armstrong

Lebanon County's Part in the Revolutionary War p. 393

John Barnett

Lebanon County's Part in the Revolutionary War p. 393

Simon Duey

John Hetrick Pension S22122

John Garberich

John Bickel Pension S22122

Adam Harper

Pennsylvania Archives Series 5, Volume 7, p. 530

John Hetrick

John Hetrick Pension R4843

William Hill

Lebanon County's Part in the Revolutionary War Page 393

Jonas Larue

Mohn, V. "Shadows of the Rhine along the Tulpehocken" Volume 2

Jacob Lehman

John Bickel Pension S22122

Anthony Long (Song)	John Hoover Pension S4402
Michael Myers	John Hoover Pension S4402
Joseph McFarling	John Hetrick Pension R4843

APPENDIX "D"

PENSION APPLICATION OF JOHN BICKEL S22122

State of Pennsylvania
County of Lebanon

On the _____ day of March 1833 personally appeared in open court before the judge of the court of common pleas, now sitting, John Bickel Esquire, a resident of Swatara Township, in the county and state aforesaid, aged eighty years the second day of May last, who being first duly sworn according to law doth on his oath making the following declaration in order to obtain the benefit of the act of congress passed June 7, 1832.

That he entered the service of the colonies in he Revolutionary War in Captain Thomas Coppenhafer's company on the 2nd day of January A.D. 1777 marched from Jonestown to Philadelphia, thence to Trenton, thence to Princeton, thence to Rocky Hill, thence to Princeton again, and was there discharged by General Putnam from militia duty and returned home, after having served a tour of duty for two months as ensign. about the 1st of September A.D. 1777 I made another tour of militia duty, marched as ensign to Featherbro Hill near Germantown, was present at the battle of Germantown, Brandywine, and served my two months in Captain Amos Green's company, under the command of Colonel Rogers. I was discharged and returned home again. I served a third tour of two months against the Indians as ensign. We were ordered to rendezvous at Greensville in East Hanover Township, Dauphin county, then Lancaster County and state aforesaid - our Captain Thomas Coppenhafer did not come, and I was an ensign the company and had received my appointment and commission as such in August 1777 and it bears date the 31st of July 1777 which I have exhibit in court. Signed by Thomas Wharton _____ President and countersigned by T. Matlock secretary. And in the summer following _____ August 1778 marched on my third tour of two months as an ensign. I then acted as Captain and marched the company under the command of Colonel Hartley and Major Eichelberger to Sunbury. Did all the duties of a captain but never received a commission as such - I remained out this tour three months and was part of the time, from 6 to 8 weeks stationed at Fort Jenkins on the North Branch of the Susquehanna River about 30 miles above the junction of the North and West branches. I never saw an Indian on this tour but we were in pursuit of them. I was again discharged in the town of Sunbury on the said river by Colonel (I think) Butler and returned again to Jonestown in the County of Lebanon, aforesaid, then Lancaster County and there I have lived ever since except a part of the _____ I lived in Hanover Township, in the said county, about a mile from Jonestown. I have no documentary evidence of my discharge but I have the commission appointing me an ensign of a company of foot in the sixth battalion of militia in the County of Lancaster. That he knows of no other person whose testimony he can procure who can testify to his services except Frederick Becker, John Gerberich and Jacob Lehman. He hereby relinquishes every claim whatever to a pension or annuity except the present and declares that his name is not on the pension roll of the agency of any state.

I served ten months as ensign and three months as captain.

Sworn and subscribed in open)
court the day and year aforesaid)

Adam Ritscher clk.   John Bickel

The following questions were propounded to John Bickel Esquire an applicant for the benefit of the act of Congress passed 7 June 1832, by the court at the time of filing his declaration:

First -	Where and in what year were you born? I was born in Bethel Township in the County of Lancaster and state aforesaid on the 2nd day of May A.D. 1752.
Second -	Have you any record of your age and if so where is it? I have it under my own father's hand. It is a leaf out of the family bible and I have it here in court.
Third -	Where were you living when called into service; where have you lived since the Revolutionary War; and where do you now live? I lived at Hanover Township about a mile from Jonestown, where I have lived and in Jonestown ever since the Revolutionary War and I now live at Jonestown as mentioned in my declaration.
Fourth -	How were you called into service; were you drafted, did you volunteer or were you a substitute? And if a substitute for whom? I was called into service under the militia system. I was drafted and served every time I was drafted. I was out four times - the last time I was only out ten days and was discharged and this I have not mentioned in my declaration.
Fifth -	State the names of some of the regular officers who were with the troops where you served; such continental and militia regiments as you recollect and the general circumstances of your service. I saw General Washington often while in Jersey and knew him - General (Charles) Lee, General (Israel) Putnam, Colonel Cox

- I knew more of them but I have forgotten their names. I do not recollect the names of the regiments and have very little recollection of the circumstances. I knew General DeHass and Colonel Hussicker who fled to the enemy at the battle of Princeton which created much excitement - the rest I have already stated in my declaration.

Sixth -   Did you ever receive a discharge from the service, and if so by whom was it given and what has become of it?
I got a written discharge from Major Latjah (Latcha) but what has become of it I know not. I cannot find it for the first tour for the other tours we got no written discharges. We only called in rank and the Muster Roll was called over and we were discharged.

Seventh -   State the names of the persons to whom you are known in your present neighborhood, and who can testify to your veracity and their belief of your service as a soldier of the Revolution. The only persons I now can recollect are Frederick Becker, John Gerberich and Jacob Lehman, the last named person is sick and unable to be in court and therefore I have taken his deposition but the other two are in court, Valentine Shoufler and Dr. William Wood.

John Bickel was born May 2, 1752 in Bethel Township, in Lancaster County. He lived in Hanover Township about 1 mile from Jonestown in 1777. He died on February 28, 1842 and is buried in the graveyard of the German Reformed Church at the corner of King and Queen Streets, Jonestown Pennsylvania (Shadows of the Rhine Along the Tulpehocken, Volume 2, by Viola K. Mohn). At this time the parents of John Bickel have not been determined, but he appears to be related to Tobias Bickel, somehow. Tobias Bickel was a near neighbor to the Copenhavers and sold a house to Simon Copenhaver in 1768. The house is still standing and is occupied. It is in Meyerstown, Pennsylvania.

APPENDIX "E"

JOHN GERBRICH AFFIDAVIT FROM
PENSION APPLICATION OF JOHN BICKEL S22122

Lebanon County ss

Before me Joel Spyker Esquire one of the Justices of the Peace in and for Lebanon County came John Gerbrich who on his solemn oath did say that he had served a tour of duty in the Revolution War, in Captain Thomas Copenhaver's company under the command of Abraham Lachar (Latcha), Major, that they have rendezvous in Jonestown the 1st of January 1777 and marched off from Jonestown on the 2nd day of January following to Reading thence to Philadelphia, from thence to Trenton, from thence to Princeton from thence to Rocky Hill at Milston (Millstone) River in the State of New Jersey, and whereas John Bickel acted as an Insign in said Copenhaver's company we were stationed at Rocky Hill for two month and scouted almost every day seen the British Army in Brunswick where the British Army lay all that winter. Then came back again to Princeton, and there we were discharged by General Putnam in Princeton, about the middle of March in same year. Then marched to Philadelphia and delivered our rifles and blankets then marched home to East Hanover and expended about three month, until we came home again, and further saith not.

Sworn and Subscribed
Before me the 28th day
of February 1833

John Gerbrich
(Also known as
John Carvery. See
Muster Roll Appendix
"L.")

Joel Spyker

The above named John Gerbrich is unable to go to court for hiving the above evidence according as the law direct on account of sickness and other infirmity, therefore the deposition was taken at his home.

J. Spyker

In 1783? John Gerbrich (Carvery) married Catherine Latcha, the daughter of Major Abraham Latcha. They had 5 children. A few years after Catherine, his first wife, died, he married Magdalene Bender in 1801. He had 7 childern by his second wife. John died at his home on September 18, 1843 and is buried near Walmer Church in East Hanover Township.

PENSION APPLICATION OF JOHN HARKERADER
S13323

State of Virginia
Wythe County

On this twelfth day of November, 1832 personally appeared in open court before the justices of the county court of Wythe County now sitting it being a court of record, John Harkerader a resident of said County of Wythe and State of Virginia aged eighty two years who being first duly sworn according to law, doth on his oath make the following declaration in order to obtain the benefit of the Act of congress passed June 7, 1832.

That he entered the service of the United States as a volunteer under the commission of a Lieutenant on the 1st day of August 1775 that being the date of said commission of a company of riflemaen in the Second Battalion of Associators in the County of Lancaster in the State of Pennsylvania which said commission was to continue in force until revoked by the assembly or by the present or any succeeding committee of safety and bears the seal of the state and signed by order of the assembly John Morton speaker which said commission is inspected by the said court and believed to be genuine and that he served under said commission as lieutenant the term of two months under the following named officers. Thomas Copenheifer Captain, Major Abraham Latcher (Latcha) that he was at the time of entering the service aforementioned a resident of the County of Lancaster in the State of Pennsylvania, that he was marched to the State of New York and was stationed at a little town called Bergan Town (Bergen, New Jersey) opposite the City of New York where he remained until his term of service had expired which was on the 1st day of October, 1775. That he never applied for any discharge or obtained any. That he is now _____ eighty three years of age since the 1st day of October last having been born on the 1st day of October 1750.

That he went out the second time and volunteered while still a resident of the said county of Lancaster under his commission aforesaid as a Lieutenant, he thinks in the latter end of the year 1776, it being _____ a few days previous to the taking the Hessians at Trenton as he was then on his march to that place and before he got there they were taken. That he served during that tour the term of two months and some days under the following named officers Captain Jacob Stover, Major Abraham Latcha, Colonel Timothy Green who was officer - First Battalion of Riflemen of Lancaster Militia but the said Colonel Green was not out that tour. That he was marched from the said county of Lancaster first of (to) Philadelphia and from thence to the Jerseys where he was stationed at a place called Rocky Hill on Millstone River until his term of service had expired and was discharged on the 10th day of March he thinks 1777 but he received no written discharge having applied for none. That he went out the third time as a volunteer while still a resident of the said county of Lancaster under his commission of lieutenant and he thinks in the 1777 and served the terms of two months under the following named officers Captain Michael Moyer, Major William Brown that he was marched for said tour from Lancaster towards Philadelphia and stopped within 25 miles of the city and then received order from General Wansington to go down and fire on the British who were there in the City of Philadelphia which order was executed by General John Bull and the fire was returned by the British but to no effect - their shot having passed entirely over the heads of the army - that happened a few days before Christmas - he thinks in 1777 - he thinks he was discharged by General James Potter at Graham Barracks at what date precisely he does not recollect. That he went out as a volunteer on the 4th tour of duty while still a resident of the said County of Lancaster in the State of Pennsylvania under the commission of captain which said commission bears date on the 10th day of May

1780 and it bears the lesser seal of the commonwealth of Philadelphia and is signed by William Moore Vice President No. 4 and attested by "TT matlock Secretary" which appointment of captain as aforesaid is to company of foot in the Ninth Battalion of Militia in the County of Lancaster in the State of Pennsylvania and which commission was to continue in force until the said term of service by the laws of the state shall of course expired and which said commission is exhibited and inspected by the court there and believed to genuine - that he served under said commission on the 12th day of July 1780 to the 6th day of September following including two days extra pay with the allowance of five days for coming home as appears for a payroll or warrant for the pay of said Captain John Harkeraders company bearing date at Lebanon _____ day of September 1780 signed by Phillip Marstiller (Marsteller) Pay Master of Lancaster County Militia and directed to the said Captain John Harkenrader accompanied with a draft on the treasury for the sum of £362 s3 p8 that being the amount of _____ money the said company was entitled to for the service aforesaid and that he paid off the troops when they returned home to Lancaster County aforesaid for which receipts were taken of them respectfully and now shown to the court believed to be genuine together with the payroll or warrants aforesaid that he was marched from Lancaster aforesaid on his fourth tour to Northumberland County in the State of Pennsylvania and was stationed at Evansburg in said county until he returned home and was then under colonel Hunter during the term aforesaid.

That he received a certificate from Colonel John Rogers of that battalion LCM (Lancaster County Militia) certifying that the said Captain John Harkenrader had served in the character of captain of that company of the 1st Battalion of Lancaster County Militia and has ever behaved himself as a soldier and in due subordination to the laws of his country both civil and military and never incurred any fines whatever - certified 30 May Anno Dom 1783 signed John Rogers Colonel 1st BATN LCM and directed to all whom it may concern which is also produced in court and believed

157

to be genuine after inspection by said court. That he was born in Berks County Pennsylvania Maxatawy Township that he removed from thence to Lancaster in the same state and from thence to Wythe County in the State of Virginia where he has ever since resided - that he has no record of his age that he can resort to - that he is well known in the neighborhood in Wythe County where he resides by the following named persons Casper Yost, John Waller. He hereby relinquishes every claim whatever to a pension or annuity except the present and declares that his name is not on the pension roll of the agency of any state whatever.

Sworn and subscribed the day and year aforesaid.

John Harkerader

John Harkerader was born on October 1, 1750 in Maxatawny Township, Berks County, Pennsylvania. It was reported by Mrs. Mary Carson in a letter written to the United State War Department in 1911, that he was the son of Conrad Harkenrader. He died November 24, 1837 in Wythe County, Virginia. The pension record identifies only one child named David.

John apparently moved to Wythe County, Virginia about the same time that Captain Thomas Copenhaver moved there (1780).

APPENDIX "G"

PENSION APPLICATION OF JOHN HETRICK

R4843

State of Pennsylvania
County of Lebanon

On the 7th day of August in the year of our Lord one thousand eight hundred and thirty-seven personally appeared in open court before the judges of the court of common pleas now sitting John Hetrick a resident of East Hanover Township in the said County of Lebanon and the State of Pennsylvania aged seventy-five years one month and fourteen (days) who being first duly sworn according to law doth on his oath make the following declaration in order to the benefit of the act of congress passed the 7 June 1832.

That he entered the service of the United States under the following named officers and served as herein stated. I entered the services of the colonies in the Revolutionary War in Captain Thomas Copenhaver's company in the month of May in the year of our Lord one thousand seven hundred and seventy-five. He is not certain as to the particular time but knows that it was shortly before the taking of New York by the British troops (the British fleet arrived in New York bay June 29, 1776). His colonel was Peter Hetrich, his father. That he left home and went to McCrights (McCreights) in Hanover Township aforesaid from there they marched down to Lancaster then to the City of Philadelphia. They embarked in the city and went about thirty miles up the Delaware river, marched through Trenton to Brunswick to (Perth) Amboy; while at Amboy our time expired and many returned home with our captain, but as volunteers were wanted I remained and served until November with a number of my comrades who turned out, of whom I recollect the names of some of my companions in the service and were named, Simon Duey, Christian Stuckey, Henry Mark and Joseph McFarling. The first three died in the service and I returned home in the fall late after having served in the company Captain Crain. After I joined Captain Crain's company we marched about 14 miles farther toward New York but the place I do not recollect-think Paulus Hook. _____ we were discharged. I was in the service more than six months from the time I left home until I returned home to wit from the month of May 1776 to the month of November 1776. McFarling also never returned home but what became of him _____ in the service. That Captain Copenhaver removed to Ohio (Virginia) report says he has died. My father the colonel is also long since dead and Captain Crain came home and lived some time after the war and report say he is long since dead - I saw the British on Staten Island but never was in battle - after my return I remained in East Hanover Township and have lived ther ever since - I do not know any person now living who could testify as to my services who was out with me but my neighbor Casper Kreiser and Philip Hetrick know that I was out in the service of the Revolutionary War. He hereby relinquishes every claim whatever to a pension or an annuity except the present roll of the agency of any state. The record of my age is in the family bible on a loose piece of paper which is in the hand-writing of my father and contains the ages of the rest of his children.

Sworn and Subscribed
in open court this   Johan Hetrich
7 Augt. 1837

PENSION APPLICATION OF WILLIAM HEDRICK (HEDREIK) R4355

State of Tennessee
Sevier County

On this 6th day of March 1833 personally appeared before me Jacob Holland one of the acting justices of the court of pleas and justice _____ in and for the said County of Sevier and the State of Tennessee at his own house in the said county and state he being entirely unable to attend court by reason of old age and bodily infirmity William Hedreik a resident of the said county and state in the said County of Sevier and State of Tennessee aged 88 years who after being first duly sworn according to law doth on his oath make the following declaration in order to obtain the benefit of the act of Congress passed June the 7th 1832. That he entered the service of the United States under the following named officers and served as herein stated. He was born in Lancaster County, Pennsylvania on the 25th day of December 1744. He has no record of his age at this time he had a record in his family bible but he lost his bible some years ago. He lived in said Lancaster County, Pennsylvania at which place he volunteered for a six month tour in the fall of 1775 as he thinks under Captain Thomas Copenhaver in Major Abraham Lidrours (Latchas) regiment of militia he was a musician and played the fife. We rendezvous at Stau_____ in Lancaster County at the time last aforesaid. We marched to Philadelphia lay there some time and was joined by a considerable army but the names of the officers not recollected then we marched to Elizabeth Town and (Perth) Amboy and then to New York lay in sight of New York some time we then marched up the river and had a battle with the British in which we were defeated, the name of the battle or or the place not recollected. We_____ in the neighborhood of the battle a considerable time and marched to New York lay there sometime and then to Trenton and there crossed the Delaware River and then back to Lancaster and was there verbally discharged which he thinks was in the spring of 1776. He served at this time six months. He may be mistaken as to the dates and the particulars of his tour but is certain he served six months at this time. He had a stroke of the palsey a few months ago which has so impaired his speech that is with great difficulty he can make himself understood. Again while living in said Lancaster County, Pennsylvania some time in the summer of 1776 as he thinks in the said County of Lancaster he enlisted for eighteen months under Captain Grubb (his christian name not recollected) in the 5th or 6th regiment of the Pennsylvania line of infantry as riflemen as he thinks. The name of the colonel that commanded him not recollected. He was the greater part of the time under the command of General Washington. He thinks he was enlisted by a man by the name of Armstrong his christian name not recollected nor his grade. He thinks he was called Doctor Armstrong. They marched to Philadelphia and then to Trenton. He was in the Battle of Trenton (December 26, 1776) and in the Battle of Princeton (January 3, 1777) and in the battle of Brandywine (September 11, 1777) and also the Battle of Germantown (October 4, 1777). After then we marched to Philadelphia and was there honorably discharged. His discharge was signed by the said Captain Grub (Grubb) as he thinks but was lost many years ago. He served his full time of eighteen months at this time. He served in the whole two years for which he claims pension.

He was a fifer during the last tour of service and as such. He has lived since the revolution in the following places to wit: He continued to live in Lancaster County, Pennsylvania _____ he then moved into Sullivan County, Tennessee lived there about nineteen years he then moved to Sevier County, Tennessee and has lived there ever since. He never was drafted nor a substitute. He cannot state the name of the regular officers commanded the troops where he served nor the continental nor militia regiment farther than above stated. He never did receive a commission during the revolution. He is known in his present neighborhood _____ _____ Cunningham, John Cotter, William Cotter, Samuel, Robert C san and Aron C san. All of whom he believes would testify that he is a man of veracity and that they believe he was a revolutionary soldier and he knows of no person whose testimony he can procure who can testify as to his service. He thereby relinquishes any claim whatsoever to any pension or annuity except the present and declares that his name is not on the pension roll of the agency of any state. Sworn to and subscribed the day and year aforesaid before me.

William (X) Hedrick
(His Mark)

Jacob Holland Justice
of the court of pleas and _____

William Hedrick was born December 25, 1744 in Lancaster County, Pennsylvania the son of George Heinrich Hedrick. At this time I cannot find a relationship between these Hedricks and the family of Lieutenant Colonel Peter Hetrick although a relationship probably exists.

PENSION APPLICATION FOR JOHN HOOVER S4402

The State of Ohio
Franklin County

On this 29th day of September in the year 1832 personally appeared in open court before the court of common pleas in and for said county in the State of Ohio now sitting, John Hoover a resident of Jackson Township in said county aged seventy-seven years who being first duly sworn according to law doth on his oath make the following declaration in order to obtain the benefit of the act of congress passed June 7, 1832.

He was born at Lebanon, Lancaster County in the State of Pennsylvania on the 19th February, 1755 no record of his age in his possession. It is contained in a bible in the possession of George Pechinstone near Harrisburg, Pennsylvania. Resided in Hanover Township Lancaster County, Pennsylvania when in the summer of 1776 being then 21 years of age volunteered in the militia for three months in the company of Captain Thomas Copenhaver, Major Abraham Latshaw (Latcha), Colonel Greenwalt (Philip Greenawalt) - Number of regiment not recollected. Marched first to Philadelphia thence to Trenton, thence to Princeton thence to Ploeus Hook (Paulus Hook, New Jersey) and continued there until time expired -_____ Michael Myers and Anthony Long privates in company and leut. was at Poleus Hook when the British frigates lay at New York bay.

In December following at Lebanon, Lancaster County, Pennsylvania volunteers for three months in militia in Captain Frederick Stovers - Major Abraham Latcha marched through Reading and stationed near Middlebrook and New Brunswick. The British were lying at New Brunswick - deep snow - two _____ feet _____ continued there till time expired - could not at that time talk English and speaking it now very imperfectly. Returned to Lebanon. Has resided in Franklin County, Ohio about twenty five years and always resided at the same place in said county but the townships divided it is now Jackson - came to Franklin County from Cynthianna County, Kentucky where he resided about 9 years. Removed from Pennsylvania to Kentucky, never received any written discharge.

He has no documentary evidence and knows of no person who can testify to his services.

He hereby relinquishes all claims whatever to pension or annuity except the present and declares that his name is not on the pension roll of the agency of any state.

Sworn to and subscribed on the day and year aforesaid.

John (X) Hoover
(His Mark)

The Daughters of the American Revolution lineage book lists John Hoover:

b.   February 19, 1755
d.   1840
m.   Margaret Smith

The pension file says: He was born at Lebanon, Lancaster County, Pennsylvania and died near Grove City, Franklin County, Ohio.

APPENDIX "J"

JOHN LEHMAN AFFIDAVIT FROM
PENSION APPLICATION OF JOHN BICKEL S22122

Lebanon County ss

Personally appeared before me the subscriber one of the justices of the peace in and for the county of Lebanon, Jacob Lehman formerly of Lancaster County now an inhabitant of Schuykill County, Pennsylvania. A man of good character and veracity and on his solemn oath deposeth and saith that he is well acquainted with John Bickel of Jonestown formerly of Lancaster County aforesaid, that the said John Bickel performed a tour of duty under the command of Captain Thomas Copenheffer's company marched from Jonestown 2, Jany 1777 to Philadelphia thence Trenton and thence to Princetown thence to Rockyhill. This deponent was in the same company and we were discharged by General Bottman (Putnam) at Princeton of our militia service in the Revolutionary War and came home to Jonestown together, about the middle of March of said year.

Sworn and Subscribed before me this
24th day of September A.D. 1832 and   Jacob Lehman
do certify that this deponent is sickly
unable to attend at Lebanon in open court

APPENDIX "K"

THE HANOVER RESOLVES

At an assembly of the inhabitants of Hanover, Lancaster County, held on Saturday, June 4, 1774, Colonel Timothy Green, chairman, to express their sentiments on the present critical state of affairs, it was unanimously resolved.

1st.   That the recent action of the Parliament of Great Britain is iniquitous and oppressive.

2nd.   That the bounden duty of the people to oppose every measure which tends to deprive them of their just prerogatives.

3rd.   That in a closer union of the colonies lies the safeguard of the liberties of the people.

4th.   That in the event of Great Britain attempting to force unjust laws upon us by the strength of arms, our cause we leave to heaven and our rifles.

5th.   That a committee of nine be appointed, who shall act for us and in our behalf as emergencies may require.

The committee consisted of Colonel Timothy Green, James Caruthers, Josiah Espry, Robert Dixon, Thomas Coppenheffer, William Clark, James Stewart, Joseph Barnett and John Rogers.

Timothy Green
Chairman

Pennsylvania in the War of the Revolution, Associated Battalions and Militia, Pennsylvania Archives, Series 2, Volume 13, Page 271, Edited by William H. Egle.

Mr. C.E. Koppenheffer of Emporium, Pennsylvania reports that the Hanover Resolutions were drafted and signed at Harper's Tavern in what is now Lebanon

County, Pennsylvania. I have not been able to confirm this, nor have I been able to locate the original document.

APPENDIX "L"

A Return of the 3rd Company of the 6th Battalion of Lancaster County shewing each mens names - respective class, also a return of those who have served in their class in the year Anno Domi 1778 and 1779.

Captain
Thomas Coppenhaver, not served having no command

Lieutenant
Abraham Latcha, not served having no command
George Beasor, not served having no command

Insign
John Bickel, served Northumberland

Drummer and Fifer
John Toops (Dubbs)   William Hedrich

Privates	Class	Remarks
Frances Alberthale (Alberdale)	6	
Nicholas Alberthal	8	
Bolzer Bomgart'r (Baumgartner)	4	
John Bomgartner	1	
Philip Bomgart'r	3	
Frederick Peasore (Bashore)	5	
Henry Peasore	3	Served Northumberland
Jacob Peasore	5	
John Peasore	2	Class A.D. 1779
Peter Peasore	1	
Nicholas Bobb	8	
John Bridbile (Brightbill)	2	
Peter Bridbile	7	

171

George Prouner (Brunner)	3	Served Northumberland
Henry Pruner	6	
John Prouner	5	
Nicholas Pruner	5	Served Lebanon
William Carpenter	1	
Lodwig Cearing	3	Class A.D. 1779

Privates	Class	Remarks
Jacob Cleaman	6	
Adam Titlor (Diebler)	6	
Nicholas Titlor	2	Class A.D. 1779
Nicholas Earhard	2	Served Northumberland
Michael Feltin	2	Served Northumberland
Peter Feltin	4	
Christopher Fox	5	Served Lebanon
John Fox	3	
Peter Fox	5	Served Lebanon
George Frank	5	
Phillip Frank	8	
Andreas Carvery (Garberich)	1	Served Mitletown
John Carvery	5	Served Lebanon
Adam Goodman (Gutman)	8	
Jacob Graff	3	
Peter Gungrey	4	
John Guntrum (Gundrum)	5	Class A.D. 1779
John Harper	4	Served Northumberland
George Hayn	4	Class A.D. 1779
George Hedrick	7	
Conrad Helm	8	
Jacob Henry	7	
Henry Hess	2	
Lodwig Klick	8	
Henry Latcha	4	Class A.D. 1779

	Class	Remarks
Henry Lowmiller	4	Served Northumberland
John Symon (Lymon)(Lehman)	2	
Adam Mark	6	
Conrad Mark	8	
Martin Mailey (Miley)	4	
Daniel Miller	3	
Jacob Moser	1	Served Mitletown
John Muser	5	
Peter Muser	8	
Christian Perkey	2	
Michael Philipey (Phillipi)	7	
James Philips	4	Served Mitletown
Joseph Pirkey (Perkey)	3	
Nicholas Poor	8	
Privates	**Class**	**Remarks**
Peter Rawer	7	
John Rayner	5	
Conrad Road	3	
Vallentine Sala	8	
Henry Shuey	6	
Nicholas Snyder	4	Served Northumberland
John Steely	1	Class A.D. 1779
Michael Straw (Stroh)	1	Served Mitletown
Bolzer Stone	7	
Henry Stone	5	Served Lebanon
Jacob Stone	2	Served Northumberland
Peter Stone	8	
Jacob Tibbine (Tibbins)	1	Served Mitletown
John Tibbing	8	
Peter Title	8	
George Unger	1	

John Walmore (Walmer)	7	
Peter Walmore	6	
Adam Weaver	6	
Daniel Weaver	1	Served Mitletown
John Weaver	6	
Adam Wentling	7	
Leonard Widowmair	2	
George Wilt	3	Served Northumberland
John Winder Jr. (Winter)	4	Class A.D. 1779
Abraham Wingard	1	
Jacob Wolff	1	Served Mitletown

The above is a true state of said company from the 24th day of April Anno 1778 until this day October 28th, 1779.

Certified by me, Thomas Coppenhaver, Captain

Pennsylvania Archives, 5th Series, Volume 7, Pages 545-547.

APPENDIX "M"

PENSION APPLICATION OF PETER BREAKBILL W46

State of Tennessee
Monroe County

On this 27th day of May 1833, personally appeared in open court before the Honorable William B. Run chancellor etc., Peter Breakbill a resident of said County of Monroe, age 73 years who being first duly sworn according to law, doth on his oath make the following declaration, in order to obtain the benefit of the act of Congress passed June 7, 1832. That he was born April 16th, 1760 in Lancaster County, Pennsylvania and resided there till he had performed all the military service he rendered, except the last two months when he volunteered _____ till he was 19 years old. He then moved to Washington County, Maryland, where he lived 12 years. He then moved to Berkley County, Virginia, and lived 5 years. He then moved to Sullivan County, Tennessee and lived about 11 years. Then into Blount County, Tennessee, and lived till about ten years ago when he moved into the said County of Monroe, where he now resides. He always served as private of infantry. In the month of July, 1776, he went into the service of the United States as a substitute for his brother Phillip Breakbill who was drafted for three months. He served in Captain Thomas Cuppenhaver's Company, under Abraham Latcher (Latcha), Major and Colonel Greenwald (Greenawalt). The said company marched from Lancaster County, Pennsylvania to Philadelphia, where they remained in barracks three or four weeks. The barracks (enclosing four acres with brick) were full of men, but who command them he does not know. He, with said company, then went up the Delaware River in a schooner, to Trenton, stayed there one day, then marched on towards New York, staying one day at Brunswick and three days at Amboy, from Amboy marched to New Warrick thence to Bergentown in sight of New York. There they joined a large army of militia under whose command he cannot remember, except that Greenwald (Greenawalt) was Colonel. He stayed at Bergentown and Paulus Hook until his three month term expired. He received a discharge signed by Colonel Greenwald (Greenawalt) which is lost. He was engaged in no battles, except that the British piping up the North River with the Roebuck and two other ships cannonaded the fort which fire the fort returned. While applicant was at Paulus Hook the British took New York.

Very shortly afterward in November, 1776, he went into the service as a substitute for his Uncle Peter Breakbill, who was drafted for a term of three months. He marched under the same captain and major as he did before and under Colonel Peter Hedrick. He marched from said Lebanon (Lancaster) county to Readingtown, thence to Ellentown — Brunswick in New Jersey, remaining there a week or more, from Brunswick they were ordered back to Trenton to take the Hessians. There they fell in with a large body of militia, and the flying camp — under what commander he cannot remember. They took a large number of Hessians - perhaps 1,500 or 2,000 — and took them on to Lancaster and guarded them in the barracks till appplicant's term of three months expired. He received a discharge signed by Colonel Hedrick which is lost.

In July 1777, applicant was drafted for three months. He went from said Lancaster County under Captain Casely, Major Daniel Bradley and Colonel (he thinks John) Green. He marched from Lebanon to Reading, thence to Bethlehem on Delaware River. They remained on the river some time. There was a great body of militia there who commenced building a fort. He was then put on a spy guard and marched up the river to a little town under the Blue Mountain. There he and those with him stayed till after the battle of Brandywine. They were then ordered to Little Brandywine where there was an army of militia — under whose command he does not know. There he remained till his term expired and he was discharged. His discharge signed by Colonel Green he has long since lost. Was in no battles.

In the month of October, 1778, a wagon belonging to Adam Harber and two horses belonging to applicant's father, and two belonging to his uncle, were pressed into service of the Continental Army by Captain Valentine Shouffler, wagonmaster. The Captain said that if a wagoneer was furnished, he should receive soldier's pay. Applicant, in order to take care of the horses, volunteered as wagoneer. He supposes the wagon and horses were picked for three months as he served out that term and received a discharge from Captain Shouffler; wagonmaster which is lost. He was engaged the three months in hauling iron from Bethlehem to Lancaster and other places and in hauling baggage, lumber, etc.

In June, 1781 or 1782, when applicant lived in Washington County, Maryland he volunteered in Captain Amos Davis' company to take prisoner a large number of Tories, who were regularly organizing themselves in a hostile manner. The Tories, assembled and made their arrangements in a laurel thicket where applicant and those with them found their papers which showed that they were regularly enrolled and sworn. They took prisoners all they could of those found enrolled; and carried them to Fredericktown, Maryland, and they were put in the barracks. Seven, he thinks, were hung at Fredericktown. He was in service this time upwards of two months and received no discharge. In all he served 14 months.

He has a record of his age, which he got in Lebanon Township, Lancaster County, Pennsylvania in 1791 from the church book —

The following persons are at present his neighbors to whom he is best known and who can testify to his veracity and their belief in his services as a soldier of the Revolution viz. Samuel Edington — John Wolfe — James A. Haire - John Dyer. He has no documentary evidence and knows of no person whose testimony he can procure who can testify to his service. He relinquishes every claim whatever to a pension or annuity except the present and declares that his name is not on the pension roll of the agency of any state.

Sworn to and subscribed the day and year aforesaid

James A. Coffin C & M

Peter Breakbill

We, Jason Matlock, a clergyman and John Dyer, both citizens of the said county of Monroe hereby certify that we are well acquainted with Peter Breakbill who has subscribed and sworn to the foregoing declaration - that we believe him to be 73 years of age; that he is reputed and believed in the neighborhood where he resides to have been a soldier of the revolution and that we concur in the opinion sworn and subscribed the day and year aforesaid.

Jason Matlock
John (X) Dyer
James A. Coffin   C & Master

And the said court do hereby declare their opinion after the investigation of the matter and after putting the interrogations prescribed by the war department that the above named applicant was a revolutionary soldier and served as he states and the court further certifies that it appears to them that Jason Matlock who has signed the preceding certificate is a clergyman - resident in said county of Monroe and that John Dyer who has also signed the same is a resident in the same county and state, and is a credible person and that their statement is entitled to credit.

W. B. Ruse

Chancellor

I, James A. Coffin, clerk and master of the chancery court held at Madisonville, Tennessee do hereby certify that the foregoing contains the original proceeding of the said court in the matter of the application of Peter Breakbill for a pension.

5-27-1833
James A. Coffin, Clerk & Master

APPENDIX "N"

STATEMENT OF JOHN GLONINGER CONCERNING HIS

MILITARY AND PUBLIC SERVICE FROM PENSION

APPLICATION W-2785

John Gloninger was born in Donegal Township, Lancaster County, on the 19th day of Sept. 1753. His parents were Philip Gloninger and his wife Barbara. He was baptized in early infancy and, at a suitable age, after a course of instruction in the principles of the Christian religion, was admitted to the Holy communion, and received as a member of the German Reformed Church.

On the 23rd of November 1784 he intermarried with Catherine Orth, daughter of Adam Orth Esq. and his wife Catherine. Their union was blessed with four sons, of whom three have departed this life. His character, as generally known, was that of an upright and honorable man he filled various stations, both civil and military. At an early age, in the year 1776, he entered the service of his country, during the Revolutionary War, and was engaged in the Battle of Staten Island and Trenton, when the Hessian troops were taken prisoners. He was also engaged in the campaign against the Indians in the northwestern parts of Pennsylvania. During the greater part of the Revolutionary War, he was engaged in active service, appointed to several military offices, and experienced a variety of hardships and sufferings. Shortly after the termination of the Revolutionary War, he was elected as Justice of the Peace for Lancaster County, and to the office of colonel of the militia. He was one of the few remaining well known members of the convention which framed the constitution, or form of government of his state. He was a member of the legislature of this state, was also a member of Congress of the United States; and for more than 40 years, Associate Judge of the County Court. So great was the confidence of the people in him, that from his younger years, to a very advanced age, he was continually kept in various offices, which he, as is well known, filled with diligence and fiedlity.

This is to certify that the foregoing is a true and correct translation of a paper in the German language, and in the handwriting of the late John Gloninger Esq. And I also further certify that I was at the funeral of the said John Gloninger, and that he was generally esteemed in this place as a Revolutionary soldier, and at his death as a last token of respect for his services in defence of the liberties of the country, was buried with the honors of war.

William G. Ernst V.D.U.

Lebanon, Penn. July 21st, 1893

APPENDIX "O"

RETURN OF CAPTAIN KOPPENHAFFER'S COMPANY, YORK CO., PENNSYLVANIA MILITIA

FEBRUARY THE 5TH, 1782 (c.)

Captain
Simon Koppenhaver

Lieutenant
Jacob Gotwald

Ensign
Phillip Benadick

Sert.
Michael Koppenhaver
Andrew Gotwald
Andrew Hack (Haek)

Corporals
Andrew Coller
Frederick Eresman (Erisman)
Adam Lichenberger

Privates

Class 1st

Phillip Snider
Killian Lichenberger
Jacob Bohne
Conrad Cline
Samuel Day
Isaac Brenaman
Phillip Ament

Andrew Lang
John Kiegh
Jacob Bixler
Ludwick Rigble
John Cline
Jacob King
Casper Knap

Mathias Backer
John Ringer

Jacob Ginder
Adam Edinger
Hennery Roth
Michael Cline
Baltzer Koller
Nicolass Snider
John Gerhard
Jacob Weltz
Fredrick Hack (Haek)

Petter Knap
Jacob Weever
John Rieff
Christian Bixler
Phillip Moore
Adam Shenck
Christian Keller
Aberham Lieb

Ludwich Shindle
Michael Melhorne
Davald Gross
Samuel Gross
George Glingenman
William Riess
George Leabenston

Conrad Snider
Joseph Koller
Jacob Knap
George Hackler
Hennery Kolp   (Wenicker)
Mickael Kolp

Phillip Kunkel

2nd Class
  Conrad Ensminger
  Andrew Smith
  Martin Kopphaver
  George Wogans
  Daniel Stricker
  Jacob Kopp
  Christian Miller
  Jacob Kopp, Junr.
  George King

3rd Class
  Mickael Triber
  Hennery Orth
  John Shriber
  Jacob Snider
  James Bridess
  George Elgenfritz
  Nathan Paub
  John Motz

4th Class
  Michael Shriber
  John Rosenbaum
  Adam Miller
  John Ginder
  Jacob Eresman
  Jacob Miller
  Conrad Seyler

5th Class
  Baltzer Rudysell
  Yost Shultz
  John Snell
  Hennery Wenicher

  William Roperts

Vallentin Kolman
John Sharp
Nicolass Day, Junr.
Andrew Potter (Rotter)
John Humberichauser

Ropert Jones
Ludwick Triber
Jonas Rudysell
Jacob Hoffman
Petter Moore

6th Class

Adam Quickel
Adam Wild
George Lickenberger
John Fetter (Fettro)
Michael Ringer
Jacob Miller
Vallentin Wild
George Miller
John Grabill
Vallentin Koller

Mickael Edinger
Mickael for Cana
(fon Cana)
George Phillip Shultz
Hennery Seyler
Petter Kopp
Fridrick Shindle
Jacob Braune
Daniel Flory
Aberham Bruehard
(Bruckard)

7th Class

Jacob Hackler (Haekler)
Petter Ellenberger
Jacob Snider
Conrad Ginder
Christiam Moore
John Miller
David Bruchard (Bruckard)

Christian Bixler
John Rudysell
John Kolherr (Kollierr)

Petter Snider
Martin Frey
Yost Harbaugh

8th Class

Vallentin Bohne
Petter Long
Joseph Bixller
Jacob Klingenman
Samuel Miller
John Hyde
George Gross

Casper Ligtenber
John Miller
Petter Shultz
Andrew Gross (Grass)
Phillip Jacob King
Fredrick Hoffman
Andrew Harskey
(Hershey)

183

A true return of Captain Simon Koppenhaffers Company, February the 8th, 1783.

SM. ASHTEN, Majer

This appendix is taken from the <u>Pennsylvania Archives</u>, 6th Series, II, 655-657 which was prepared from the original in the archives division, Pennsylvania State Library. Spelling variations are taken from Red Series, Volume 1, York County, Pennsylvania in the American Revolution, a source book, compliled by Henry James Young, 1939.

APPENDIX "P"

MUSTER ROLL OF CAPTAIN SIMON COPENHAVER'S COMPANY

3D. COMPANY [PROBABLY 2ND BATTALION]

YORK CO., PA. MILITIA (1777, 1778)

Simon Copenhaver Senr. Captain
Michael Shriver   1 Lieutnt.
Andrew Smith   2 Lieutnt.
Jacob Gotwalt   Ensign

1 Class

1. James Smith
2. Michael Pence
3. Philip Windermier
4. Geor. Humerichhauser
5. John Crawl
6. Jacob Evesmann
7. Jacob Shindall
8. Henry Bann
9. Leonard Michal

2d. Class

10. Geor. Bonig
11. Jacob Graff
12. Fredrick Hack
13. John Cofman Junr.
14. Conrad Ensminger
15. Geor. Witerright
16. Philip Rindisell

3d. Class

17. Reynard Klin
18. Nathn. Worley
19. Henry Arth
20. Peter Witeright
21. Philp. Will
22. John Shriver
23. Peter Shultz

4 Class

24. Henry Ness
25. Peter Pense
26. Danl. Worley
27. John Ridinger
28. Andw. Hash
29. Philip Hoffman
30. John Sheriff

5 Class

31. Andw. Writer
32. Stephen Ridinger
33. John Kintzel
34. Christn. Kintzel
35. John Shram
36. Jones Rydesilley
37. John Humierichhauser
38. Godfrey King

6th. Class

40.[sic] Jacob Coffman
41. Jacob Worley
42. John Willis
43. Feltin Wilt
44. Michl. Sprimitil
45. Geo. Miller
46. John Kribiel

7th. Class

47. John Fry

48.	John Smith
49.	Nichols. Hertoz
50.	John Herman
51.	Fredrk. Shindel
52.	Jacob Godwalt

8th Class

53.	James Worley
54.	Andw. Harshy
55.	Andw. Reece
56.	Saml. Wilt
57.	Peter Long
58.	Jacob Hufft
59.	John Coofman
60.	Simn. Coppenhaver Junr.

Total 60 [Endorsed: this Company is Done]

This list was reproduced from "York County Pennsylvania in the American Revolution", pages 518-520, a source book compiled by Henry James Young, Volume I, 1935.

APPENDIX "Q"

[From a photostat in the possession of The Historical Society of York county; the original is one of the J. Horace Rudy Collection of militia returns presented to the Pennsylvania State Library by the Daughters of the American Revolution. Although it is undated, internal evidence assigns it to the period 1777-1779.]

Kaptin [Simon] Kopenhoffer
erster leitenam Michael Schreiber
zweyder leitnem andreas Schmit
[Schunet ?] Jun.
insein Jacob Gottwalt der alte

1. [Johannes Scheirff (?) - deleted] nicht fied beym boll ausgemacht [tr. unfit - removed by vote]
2. Andreas Schinerd [?] Zweyder lietnam
3. Johannes Frey 7
4. Reinhard Klein 3
5. Henrich Nes 4
6. Petter Benes 4 Excused
7. Jacob Kauffman 6
8. Schim Worle 8
9. Jacob Worle 6
10. Phillib Wachner [Wagner] 6
11. Nedan Worle 3
12. Danniel Worle 4
13. Anderes Ritter 5
14. Johanes Reittinger 4
15. Steffe Teittinger 5
16. Jacob Wachener 3
17. Johanes Keintzle 3
18. Christ. Kintzle 5
19. Johanes Schinerd 7
20. Schiny Schinerd 1

21. Johanes Wils 6
22. Ifan Griffy 2
[23.   Baltzer Ruttysiel 7 - deleted]
24.   Andras Herschy 8
25.   Hannes Schreierle 3 nicht fiedt [tr. unfit]
26.   Michal Schreiver erster leitnam
27.   Andtress Krass 8
28.   Pette Schultz der taglener [tr. day-laborer] 3
29.   Simon Kobhaffer Kaptin
30.   Simon Kobhoffer der Jung
31.   Samel Wilt 8
32.   Falendein Wilt 8
33.   Andres Heck 4
34.   Petter Lang 8
[35.   Gerg Hufft - deleted]
36.   Gorg Romich 2
37.   Jacob Hufft 8
[38.   -torn] Jacob Graff 2
39.   Mickel Benes 1 bezalt [tr. paid - a substitute ?]
40.   Nickalaus Henes 7
41.   Mickel Sprenenckel [Sprenckel] 6
42.   Phillib Windermayer 1
43.   Jones Herman 7
44.   Phillib Hoffman 4
45.   Friederich Heck 2
46.   Henerich Ord 3
47.   Gerg Henerichhauss 1
48.   Petter Witterrecht 3 excusd
49.   Jacob Herman 4
50.   Geog. Witterrecht 2
51.   Hanes Carl 1
52.   Johanes Schram 5
53.   Phillib Weil 3 excusd
54.   Gorg Miller Ju[n]ge 6
55.   Jacob Ersman 1
56.   Jacob Schindel 1
57.   Friederich Schindel 7
58.   J'anes Haffman 8
59.   Johanes Haffman Ju[n]ge 2

60. Gotfried Konig 5
61. Jonas Rutysil 5
62. Phillib Ruttysil 2
63. Henerich Kan 1
64. Johannes Hunrichhauser 5
65. Jacob Gottwalt der alte [,] insein
66. Jacob Gottwalt der Junge 7
67. Johannes Kriebiel 6
68. Conrad Insmenger 2
69. Joseph Corll - deleted]
70. Lonhard Weickel

This list was reproduced from "York County Pennsylvania in the American Revolution", pages 561-563, a source book compiled by Henry James Young, Volume I, 1935.

This list is substantially the same as the list in Appendix "P" and is only included to illustrate the extreme German character of this company. Even though many of these men were 2nd or 3rd generation North Americans.

APPENDIX "R"

No. 12800 Capt. Simon Copenhaver's Pay Roll from August 10th to October the 10th 1781

		[Pay]		[Bounty]
Simon Copenhaver Capt.		£30.pd.		5.10.0
John Mapin Lieut.		25.10.pd.		
Philip Evert Ensign			15.0.0	5.10.0
Mathias Sitler Sergt.		6.pd	1.10.0	5.10.0
Andrew Smith	do.		7.10.0	3.0.0
James Burn	do.		7.10.0	3.0.0
Thomas Fullerton Corpl.		5.10.pd.		5.0.0
Frederick Erisman	do.		5.10.0	5.0.0
Andrew Gotwalt	do.	5.10.pd.		5.0.0
Michael Rester Private			5.0.0	5.10.0
John Buse	do.	0.8.4pd	4.11.8	5.10.0
Ludwig Wyer	do.		5.0.0	5.10.0
Charles Wilcox	do.	0.8.4pd	4.11.8	5.10.0
Jacob Ludwig	do.	5.pd.		5.10.0
Matthew Willis	do.	10.10pd.		
Jacob Day	do.		5.0.0	5.10.0
Peter Neorgs	do.		5.0.0	5.10.0
Martin Shrine	do.		5.0.0	5.10.0
John Croll	do.	10.10pd.		
Jacob Hyer	do.	0.8.4pd.	4.11.8	5.10.0
Philip Shindle	do.		5.0.0	5.10.0
George Keaner	do.		5.0.0	5.10.0

£85.15.0 £95.10.0

		[Pay]	[Bounty]
Amot. Brot. over		85.15.0	95.10.0
Patrick Linn Private		£0.8.4 pd. 4.11.8	5.10.0
Thomas McKirll	do.	4.pd. 1.0.0	5.10.0
William Ramsey	do.	0.8.4pd. 4.11.8	5.10.0
Samuel Dickson	do.	0.8.4pd. 4.11.8	5.10.0
Samuel Vernon	do.	5.pd.	5.10.0
George Michael	do.	5.0.0	5.10.0
Peter Sprinkle	do.	5.0.0	5.10.0
Robert Grant	do.	5.0.0	5.10.0
Lawrence Fisher	do.	5.0.0	5.10.0
Adam Plyer	do.	5.0.0	5.10.0
Abraham Kirl	do.	5.0.0	5.10.0
Patrick Gibson	do.	5.0.0	5.10.0
James Kenedy	do.	5.pd.	5.10.0
David Adams	do.	10.pd.	5.10.0
George Elias	do.	5.0.0	5.10.0
Ludwig Weyer	do.	5.0.0	5.10.0
John Buhanan	do.	0.8.4pd. 4.11.8	5.10.0
Jacob Kinter	do.	5.pd.	5.10.0
Moses Saybrooks	do.	0.8.9pd. 4.11.3	5.10.0
David Ramsey	do.	5.pd.	5.10.0
John Wertz	do.	5.0.0	5.10.0
		£159.12.11	£206.0.0

Capt. Simon Copenhaver's Pay Roll Continued

		[Pay]	[Bounty]
Amot. Brot. over		159.12.11	206.0.0
John Neaf Private		5.0.0	5.10.0
Daniel Wertz	do.	5.0.0	5.10.0
Peter Wertz	do.	5.0.0	5.10.0
John Anderson	do.	5.0.0	5.10.0
Barnet Reed	do.	5.0.0	5.10.0
William Wilson	do.	5.0.0	5.10.0
Jacob Kuhn	do.	5.0.0	5.10.0
James Thompson	do. 0.6.8pd.	4.13.4	5.10.0
George Hines	do.	5.0.0	5.10.0
Elix Cummins	do.	5.0.0	5.10.0
John Rensher	do.	5.0.0	5.10.0
Michael Miller	do. 4.pd.	1.0.0	5.10.0
Jacob Long	do.	5.0.0	5.10.0
Thomas Brooks	do. 5.pd.		5.10.0
William Blackburn	do.	5.0.0	5.10.0
Henry Rudisill	do.	5.0.0	5.10.0
Robert Parks	do. 5.pd.		5.10.0
Charles Stephenson	do. 8.pd.		2.10.0
Adam Ross	do.	5.0.0	5.10.0
John McDonnell	do.	5.0.0	5.10.0
John McKenney	do.	5.0.0	5.10.0
		£245.6.3	£318.10.0

Capt. Simon Copenhaver's Pay Roll Continued

		[Pay]	[Bounty]
Amot. Brot. over		245.6.3	318.10.0
William Willis Private£7.5.6pd.			3.4.6
Michael Kuhn	do.	5.0.0	5.10.0
Philip Stombach	do.	5.0.0	5.10.0
Conrad Lorlach	do.	5.0.0	5.10.0
John Appley	do.10.10pd.		
Adam Kuhn	do.	5.0.0	5.10.0
Jacob Isenhart	do.5. pd.	5.10.0	
Philip Overdur	do.	5.0.0	5.10.0
		£270.6.3	£354.14.6
			270.6.3
		Entd. WBAAA	

£625.0.9

Page 374

This appendix was copied from "York county, Pennsylvania in the American Revolution", a source book Red Series Volume I compiled by Henry James Young, 1939.

APPENDIX "S"

PENSION APPLICATION OF THOMAS COPENHAVER
R2311

State of Missouri
County of Lincoln

On this sixth day of May personally appeared in open court before the Justice of the County Court now sitting Thomas Copenhaver a resident of Lincoln County and State of Missouri aged 71 years who being duly sworn according to law on oath make the following declaration in order to obtain the benefit of an act of Congress passed June 7th A.D. 1832.

That he entered the service of the United States under the following named officers and served as therein stated. The infirmities of age and lapsed time have destroyed all recollection of the field officers names. William Glaves (Gleaves) was my captain. I entered the service in the month of August in the year 1780. Our tour of service was for two months at which time the company was discharged. We was in no engagement during the time I resided in Montgomery County, Virginia. When I entered the service which was as a volunteer, we rendezvoused at the lead mines in Montgomery county Virginia from there we marched into North Carolina to Hoosier Town, when I was taken sick and left behind. We served with no regular troops, having volunteered in a call from the proper authority to go against and keep in subjection the tories who at times had nearly over ran North Carolina. The company I belonged to was engaged in North Carolina where I cannot say as I was left behind sick as before stated. Many of the men came back by the way of Hoosier Town with whom I returned home. I again entered the service in the fall of 1780. Colonel William Preston and Major Joseph Cloyd was my field officers and Captain Robert Buckhannan (Buchannan) and 1st and 2nd

Liertenants William Campbell and Robert Davis was my company officers. We entered for three months as volunteers and was discharged about the time of the Battle of Guilford Court House. I was in one engagement this tour which was at Haw River (Haw River Battle is also called Battle of Allamance Creek in some books.) with a part of Cornwallis's army some three or four days after we was discharged. I know of no particular circumstance that would tend to give light on the subject of my service save one. When in our march a man of the name or Carr who deserted and gave Tarlten (Tarleton) notice of our coming or they would have been completely surprised by us. That I have no documentary evidence that I know of nor no person save one James Davis, a nephew of one of our lieutenants who can testify to my service. The affidavit of Mr. Davis I have inserted here.

State of Missouri
County of Lincoln

James Davis having been duly sworn according to law deposith and saith that he is personally acquainted with Thomas Copenhaver the applicant that to his certain knowledge said applicant served the last tour as stated by him in his declaration as he lived a near neighbor to him at that time and that he has every reason to believe that he served as before stated by the applicant. He also knows of said applicant having went out at several times against the Indians after the war with Great Britian and further the deponent saith not.

JAMES DAVIS

Sworn and Subscribed to in
Open Court May 6th 1834

Francis Parker Clerk

I also made two excursions against the Indians about
the time peace was made with the British they being at that
time very bad coming into the settlements committing
depredations killing men women and children.

Captain Robert Davis was my officer commanding
in each of the tours. The time I served against the Indians I
cannot say precisely, perhaps two months.

Question 1st Where and what year were you born?

Answer   I was born in Lancaster County, Pennsylvania
on the 16th day of July A.D. 1763.

Question 2 Have you any record of your age and if so
where is it?

Answer   I have a record of my age at home made by
my father in German.

Question 3 Where were you living when called into
service? Where have you lived since the
Revoluntionary War and where do you now
live?

199

Answer   I resided in Montgomery County, Virginia
            when called into service and continued to
            reside there until 1831 when I removed to
            Lincoln County, Missouri where I now
            reside.

Question 4 How were you called into service? Were you
            drafted? Did you volunteer or were you a
            substitute and if so for whom?

Answer   I entered as a volunteer all the different times
            I was in the service of my country.

Question 5 State the names of some of the regular officers
            who were with the troops when you served,
            such continental and militia regiments as you
            can recollect and the general circumstances
            of the case.

Answer   We were never attached to any regular troops
            to the best of my recollection. My service was
            altogether against the tories on the frontier
            of North Carolina near Virginia. There was
            never more than one regiment together at
            least none was ever attached to ours if my
            memory does not fail me. As to the
            circumstances of the case they are pretty
            much as I have already stated. The tories at
            that time had nearly over ran all North
            Carolina, troops was continually being called
            for from Virginia to keep them in subjection.

Question 6   Did you ever receive any discharge from the
              service and if so by whom was it given and
              what has become of it?

Answer   I never received any discharge at the time of
              my first tour. I was sick at the time my
              company was discharged. On my other tour
              the regiment was discharged generally no
              one receiving an individual discharge.

_____

Question 7   State the names of persons to whom you are
              known in your present neighborhood and
              who can testify as to your character for
              veracity and good behavior and your service
              as a soldier of the revolution.

Answer   I am acquainted with Judge M. Garlan, Col.
              Watts, Captain Stenart, Gabriel Reeds,
              Nicholas Wells and William Beard.

        I hereby relinquish every claim whatever to a
pension or an anuity except the present and declare that my
name is not on the pension or agency of any state.
        Sworn and subscribed to the day and year aforesaid
in open court.

                                    His
Francis Parker Clerk   Thomas X   Copenhaver
                                    Mark

APPENDIX "T"

PENSION APPLICATION OF THOMAS WILT (W3322)

State of Pennsylvania   )
)
Bedford County   )

On this 25th day of November A.D. 1834 personally appeared in open court before the Honorable Alexander Thornson President_____ His associated judges of the Court of Common Pleas of Bedford County now sitting, Thomas Wilt a resident of Greenfield Township in said County of Bedford and State of Pennsylvania aged seventy-seven years and upwards, who being first duly sworn according to law, doth on his oath make the following declaration, in order to obtain the benefit of the act of Congress passed June 7th 1832.

That he entered the service of the United States under the following named officers, and served as herein stated.

That some time in the _____ September A.D. 1777 he was drafted in the militia of York County Pennsylvania, under Captain Kurtz, Colonel Anderson and General Potter, that from York they marched to Chester County where they were marched to the White Horse where they continued for about a week, when they were ordered to break up their encampment and to remove to a place a short distance from the White Horse known as the New Square; that they remained at New Square probably two weeks, and marched thence to Farmer's mill about four miles from Germantown where, and at which place and in the neighborhood of which they remained a considerable time, but cannot say how long; that whilst there they had several skirmishes with the Britain and Hessians, one of which he remembers particularly. It took place on or near the farm of one Robison, a Quaker, who had given information of the place of their encampment, in consequence of which, the enemy came upon them, but were repulsed. In this skirmish two men of applicants company, one of whom was in his mess, were killed. That after this they were marched up the Reading Road to a place called the Trap, where there was an encampment under Generals Bull and Armstrong, and at which place they were mustered and discharged. He was out this tour two months. That during said time besides the officers already named he remembers General Washington whom he has frequently seen.

That after the return from said tour and about the middle of harvest following (Fall 1778) he was again drafted in the militia of York County, being in class number four. That he was kept a few days after the time he was to march by a Mr. Sherman for whom he was reaping, and was then sent off with five others under the direction of Mr. Sherman and Colonel Slagle to Major Bailey of York who supplied them with arms and directed them to their company which was stationed four miles below York guarding the Prisoners captured with Burgoyne. That they joined their company under the command of Captain Forrey and continued in said service of guarding the prisoners until the end of the time for which he was drafted viz two months - that at the end of said time applicant's father was drafted as belonging to the 5th Class of the Militia of York County, and sent to take the place of those whose terms had expired, and that as applicant's father was an old man, he (applicant) agreed to serve as a substitute for him, and accordingly entered the company of Captain Copenhaver and served two months as before guarding said prisoners. That afterwards in the Winter of 1781 and 82, he went out as a substitute for Martin Stohenseifer who had been drafted in the militia of Frederick County, Maryland. That he was under the command of Captain Shields and was engaged nearly two months in guarding the prisoners captured with Cornwallis, that near the end of the time he marched with the prisoners from Frederick to York, about two miles from which place they delivered up the prisoners to other guards waiting to receive them. That after the prisoners were delivered up they marched back to Fredricktown and gave up their arms and were discharged. He was out two months.

Applicant further states that he was born in Berks County, Pennsylvania in the year 1757 and that he has a copy of the record of his age in his possession. That at the time he was called into the service, which was twice by draft and twice as a substitute he was residing with his father whose farm was on the line between the states of Pennsylvania and Maryland and the Counties of York and Frederick - that after the Revolutionary War he went to Baltimore and remained there nearly two years, then returned to his father's and lived with him about a year, then married and resided in Frederick County, Maryland four years after which he removed to McConnells _____
Bedford County, Pennsylvania and resided there five years, then removed to Huntingdon County where he resided five years and from which he removed to his present residence in Bedford County where he has resided ever since, about thirty-one years.

That he never had a commission.

Had two discharges, one from Captain Forrey and one from Shields, both lost.

That Jacob Longenfelter and Abraham Dively can testify as to his character for veracity and their belief of his services and that John Adams can testify as to a part of his services.

That he hereby relinquishes every claim whatever to a pension or annuity except the present and declares that his name is not on the pension list roll of the agency of any state.

Sworn and subscribed the)   His
)   Thomas X Wilt
Day and year aforesaid   )   Mark

205

APPENDIX "U"

ANDREW HUBER AFFIDAVIT FROM PENSION
APPLICATION
OF JOHN GLONINGER W2785

State of Pennsylvania)
                      :ss
Lebanon County   )

      Personally appeared before me the subscriber a justice of the peace in and for the County of Lebanon aforesaid Andrew Huber a resident of said county and a soldier of the Revolutionary War, who doth depose and say upon oath that he is now in the seventy seventh year of his age - That he marched from the town of Lebanon through Reading and Newark to New York in Captain Henry Baylors Company, Philip Greenawalt Colonel Pennsylvania Militia, and afterward in Colonel Glatzs (Klotzs) Regiment Flying Camp. That he continued in the service eight months - that John Gloninger also marched - at the same time from the same place to New York and was in the mess with me, and served during the whole period, as above stated, of eight months, first as a private, but was shortly after he arrived at New York appointed a corporal in which capacity he served during the remainder of the period.

Sworn and subscribed   His
before me this 4th day of   Andrew X Huber
April A.D. 1839   Mark

J.B. Hiester
Witness Present at Signing
J. Krause

APPENDIX "V"

DILMAN DAUB AFFIDAVIT FROM PENSION
APPLICATION
OF JOHN GLONINGER W2785

State of Pennsylvania)
:ss
Lebanon County   )

Personally appeared before me the subscriber a justice of the peace in and for the County of Lebanon aforesaid Dilman Daub a soldier of the Revolutionary War who doth depose and say that he is now in the seventy ninth year of his age, and a resident of Lebanon County - that in the beginning of the year seventeen hundred and seventy seven he marched from the town of Lebanon through Reading, Easton and Amboy to Long Island in the State of New York, and remained there in the service of the Revolution in Colonel Greenawalts regiment Pennsylvania Militia for a period of four months - that John Gloninger also marched from the same place to the State of New York and remained in the service of the Revolution during the whole period of four months at Long Island aforesaid, in New Jersey and along the Delaware River - that he was well acquainted with the said John Gloninger from the early part of the Revolution to the time of his death in 1836. - That he served during the whole period of the Revolution, first as a private, and afterward under various commissions and lastly as sub-lieutenant in which capacity he served to the close of the war.

Subscribed and sworn   His
before me this first day of   Dilman X Daub
April 1839   Mark

J.B. Hiester

APPENDIX "W"

VALENTINE SHOUFFLER AFFIDAVIT FROM PENSION APPLICATION OF JOHN GLONINGER W2785

State of Pennsylvania)
                                    :ss
Lebanon County   )

      Personally appeared before me the subscriber a justice of the peace in and for the county aforesaid Col. Valentine Shouffler a soldier of the Revolutionary War - who doth depose and say that he is now in the eighty seventh year of his age - that he was well acquainted with John Gloninger of Lebanon, Lebanon County, Pa. and recollects and knows well that said John Gloninger was appointed a sub-lieutenant for Lancaster County and that he acted and performed service in the Revolutionary War in that capacity to the close thereof. That he came to Northumberland County while I was there engaged with my battalion in the service of the Revolution, and brought and paid money to the troops under my command.

Sworn and subscribed
Valentine Shouffler
before me this 5th day of
April A.D. 1839

John Bickel Junior

APPENDIX "X"

ABRAHAM SEBOLT AFFIDAVIT FROM PENSION APPLICATION OF JOHN GLONINGER W2785

State of Pennsylvania)

:ss

Lebanon County   )

     Personally appeared before me the subscriber a justice of the peace in and for the county aforesaid Abraham Sebold a soldier of the Revolutionary War - who doth depose and say that he is now in the seventy eighth year of his age. That he was well acquainted with John Gloninger of Lebanon, Pa. who was also a soldier of the Revolution. That I well recollect and know that the said John Gloninger was appointed by the Supreme Executive Council a sub-lieutenant for Lancaster County and that he acted and performed service in the Revolutionary War, in said capacity of sub-lieutenant to the end of the war. That he was also in the service in the Flying Camp in the War of the Revolution under the command of Colonel Grubb.

Sworn and subscribed
Abraham Sebolt
before me this 5th day of
April A.D. 1839

John Bickel Junior

Four items of correspondence involving Christopher Kucher in June of 1780. The first three are from Series II of the Pennsylvania Archives 1780, pages 288-289 and page 324. Number four is from Volume 12 of Pennsylvania Colonial Records, page 392.

COL. THO'S EDWARDS TO CHRISTOPHER KUCHER, 1780

Lebanon, June 1st. 1780.

Dear S⁺,

Capt. Moore has resigned, and of Capᵗ. Immels District I cannot procure a return, Immel wont Serve and Capᵗ Wendle Weaver who was appointed in his room likewise declines Serving, this prevents me from sending you a return of the Officers of the Battalion in order to have commission made out for them. I am afraid we are in a fair way of getting in confusion. Capᵗ. Weiser attempted to collect Fines for Non Attendance of Exercise but received Ill Treatment and Blows in lieu of Money, and declares that he will attempt to lift the Fines unless he be properly Assisted, which I hope you will cause to be done, for you heard my short harangue to the People on the Fields, and my assurance of having the Fines regularly Collected, now should this not be done I cannot possable Serve, and shew my Face to the People with any Credit. You are well Convinced of my readiness to serve my Country to the best in my power, but nevertheless would wish to do it in such a manner as will give Honor to myself, and such who were pleased to appoint me.

I remain S⁺. with due regard,

Your Hum^le Servt
THO'S. EDWARDS Col.

Directed - The Honorable Christopher Kucher, Esq.,
Philadelphia favored Mr. Forsyth.

CHRISTOPHER KUCHER TO PRES. REED, 1780.

The Trapp on my Road home, June 2d, 1780.

Hono^{bie} Sir,
I this moment have Received the Inclosed Letter
from Col. Thomas Edwards of the Second Battalion of our
County. I Need Not say further on the subject than what
the Letter will Convey which I Think (if Right) there should
be some mode fell upon by Council to set apart as many of
the Militia for the purpose of supporting those men
appointed to collect fines from (Non attendants) as would
Effectually suport the Laws and at same time convince the
Refractory part that they are to submit to those Laws. I most
sincerely Lament that this is the Case, and most sincerely
Beg pardon if any thing herein Contained should Convey
an Idea that I would in any wise Dictate to your Excellency.

I am Hon'ble Sir,
your most ob'^t. Hum'l.
CHRISTOPHER KUCHER, S.L.L.C.

P.S. Please to Give me Your answer to the above by
the first Possible opportunity.

Publick Service
Directed, - To his Excellency Joseph Reed president of the
Supreme Executive Council of the State of Pennsylvania,
favored by Mr. John Forsyth.

COLO. CHRISTOPHER KUCHER TO PRES. REED, 1780.

Lebanon, June 15th, 1780.

Sir,

By Mr. Phillip Weiser Your Excellency will Receive the Roll of the Officers of the Second Battalion of Lancaster County Militia, To Whom You will be Pleased to Grant Commissions.

The Pressing Demands and Penetrative Requests of the well Affected People for the Collection of the Old Fines, Necessitating me to make Application for Your Excellency's Order and Direction in the Premises, to Attone the Heavy Complaints of the Good People who have allways Rendered their Personal Services in the Militia, and to Silence the Ridicule and Tantalizing of the Disaffected, who never have done any Duty, neither in Person nor in the Pecuniary Way.

Should Your Excellency be Pleased with the Recommendation of Mr. Adam Orth,* then it is hoped Your will Please to Direct him to put the Law in Execution against such as were Delinquent under the Late Militia Law, and to Prevent to Total Pernicious Consequence which will Attend the Collection of the New Fines, before the Old shall be fully Discharged.

Your Excellency will Therefore take the Premises in Consideration, and Grant the Good People Such Reasonable Satisfaction, and Enable the Present Officers to discharge the Farther Services Required of them, as Your Excellency Shall think Proper.

> I am, with due Respect,
> Your Excellency's most Obedt. Humb.

Servant,

CHRISTOPH KUCHER, S.L.L.C.

Directed,

On Public Service.

To his Excellency, Jos. Reed, President, at Philadelphia.

Favoured per Mr. Weiser.

In Council.

PHILAD'A, Monday, June 19th, 1780.

PRESENT:

His Excellency the President.

Hon'be the Vice President.

Mr. Gardner, Mr. Hambright, and
Mr. Arndt, Mr. Thompson. (now
first returned from his family.)

An order was drawn on the Treasurer in favour of
Andrew Doz, Esq'r, Commissioner of purchases for the city
of Philadelphia, for £5000 of the money emitted in pursuance
of an act of Assembly, passed the 25th day of March last,
entitled "An Act for raising the sum of one hundred
thousand pounds, &ea."

An order to Captain Isaac Roach, for the sum of
4000 dollars, for apprehending Thomas James, John
Robinson, John Farris, and William Han, four refugees from
New York, taken in Delaware Bay, agreeable to the late order
of this Board.

A letter was read from his Excellency General
Washington, dated the sixteenth instant, requesting that the
light horse of this City be ordered to proceed to camp with
all possible expedition.

A letter from Colonel Clement Biddle, Forage
master, requesting the aid of this State in his department.

A letter from Colonel Marsteller, dated the 16th
inst't, respecting the purchase of cattle, was read, and an
order was drawn in his favour for the sum of six thousand
three hundred & seventy-two pounds ten shillings, for the
purpose aforesaid.

A letter from Christopher Kucher, recommend'g Adam Orth to collect the outstanding fines on the Militia law, and inclosing a list of the officers of his Battalion.

A letter from the Hon'be Board of Admiralty Congress, praying that two or three armed Boats of this State may attend the Mercury packett ordered to cruise in the bay of Delaware.

Resolved, That the same be compiled with, and that Captain Boys do furnish two of the best of said Boats for said purpose. The Captain of the Mercury, it is expected, will return the same in good condition, accidents only excepted.

A letter from his Excellency the President of Congress, dated the 16th instant, renewing his application for Men and supplies.

APPENDIX "Z"

List of men who served under Captain Balthaser Orth in the 1st Company of the 2nd Battalion of Lancaster County Militia, probably during May of 1780.

Christian Bachman	June 18, 1758	July 14, 1838
Christiam Behm	1766	August 4, 1841
Rudolph Behm	September 5,1761	February 29, 1844
Peter Berry	Pension Application S5275	
Jacob Boehm	September 24, 1759	August 9, 1822
Christian Burcholder	February 2,1734	August 22, 1806
John Burcholder		
John Philip Carmini	December 3,1758	March 5, 1834
Samuel Etter	January 2,1758	January 15, 1840
Peter Fischer	March 6,1761	September 16, 1814
Michael Gingrich	July 23, 1753	July 11, 1838
George Hess	Pension Application W3418	
Johannes S. Imboden	October 23, 1733	July 25, 1819
Tobias Kreider	December 8,1759	July 22, 1835
Rudolph Miller	October 1,1746	November 6, 1806
Christopher Moyer	1734	August 2, 1801
Johann Orth	1760	1784
Johann Adam Orth	March 10, 1733	November 15, 1794
Gottlieb Orth	February 23, 1764	1831
Jacob J. Rohland	1759	1849
Jacob Sander	July 20, 1734	April 16, 1817
Johannes Schmidt	February 25, 1731	March 9, 1818
Lorenz Siegrist	January 15, 1731	May 18, 1825
Paul Sieg		
Daniel Stouffer		
George Troutman	May 17, 1733	March 17, 1791
John Zimmerman	April 11, 1756	March 18, 1825

APPENDIX "AA"

PENSION APPLICATION OF MICHAEL COPPENHAFFER S22690

State of Pennsylvania)
              :ss
York County   )

On this eighth day of April in the year of our Lord Eighteen Hundred and Thirty-Four, personally appeared in open court in the court of common pleas in and for the County of York, Michael Coppenhaffer a resident of Conawaga Township, York County in the State of Pennsylvania aged seventy-six years, who being first duly sworn according to law saith, and doth make the following declaration in order to obtain the benefit of the provisions made by the act of Congress passed the seventh June Eighteen Hundred and thirty-Two. That he entered the service of the United States under the following named officers and served as hereinafter stated to wit, that he entered the service at York Pennsylvania as a volunteer in the company of volunteers commanded by Yost Harbaugh on or about the first day of July Seventeen Hundred and Seventy-Six, - that he marched as a member of Capt. Harbaughs company through Lancaster to Philadelphia, that they went from there in a vessel to Trenton, New Jersey, and thence marched through N. Jersey to Amboy. From Amboy they marched to Bergen. That at Elizabeth Point he entered into the Flying Camp in the company commanded by Capt. Michael Smyser in the regiment of Col. Michael Swope for the term of six months. That he served the whole time of the six months for which he enlisted. That he has no discharge. That at the time Col. Swope was taken prisoner, he was laying sick in th neighborhood of Fort Lee. That he lived in the County of York at the time he volunteered but was a native of Lancaster County in this state, of that part now Lebanon County. That he hereby relenquishes every claim whatever to a pension or annuity except the present and declares that his name is not on the pension roll of the agency of any state and further saith not.

Michael Coppenhaffer

(In German)

APPENDIX "BB"

A LIST OF CAPTAIN BUCHANAN'S COMPANY OF MILITIA PROBABLY IN THE SPRING OF 1781

Robt. Buchanan, Capt.
Robt. Davis, 1st Lieut.
Wm. Camble (Campbell),
Wm. Calhoun, Seargt.
Robt. Black
Henry Bough
Peter Etter
John Wilson
Mickel (Michael) Staffey (Steffey)
James Davis
James Cuttin
Jacob Hetrick (Hedrick)
Wm. Hall
Stuffel (Christopher) Phillippi
Mickel (Michael) Bough
James Little
Peter Mouses (Musser)
Daniel Pruner (Brunner)
John Shannon

Peter Snavley
Joseph Cotton
Jacob Tobler (Dobler)
Joseph Davis
Samuel Davis
Joseph Atkins
Lawrence (Catron) Ketterling

Peter Kinder
William Davis
2nd Lieut.John Phillippi
Adam Shattin
Charles Blakey
Andrew Vaught
Wm. Patterson
Wm. Boyd
Robt. Cowdin (Cowden)

Exekiel (Ezekiel) Buchanan
Thomas Caswell (Cassell)
Robert Crow
Jacob Snevly (Snavely)
Nickels (Nicolas) Snider
John Fisher
Bezel Maxfield
Robt. Shannon
Wm. Calhoun
Thomas Cuphavin (Copenhaver)
Edward North
David May
Daniel Blevins
Cesey Lake
Caleb McConnudy
Isack (Isaac) Green
Joseph Alston

This company is undoubtedly the same as the company described by Thomas Copenhaver in his pension application (R2311), and the same company that marched to North Carolina and participated in two battles under the command of Colonel William Preston.

APPENDIX "CC"

August 28, 1776 The Pennsylvania Gazette
Item #59925
August 28, 1776
The Pennsylvania Gazette

Philadelphia, August 22, 1776.

FIFTY SIX DOLLARS Reward. DESERTED, this morning, from Captain Copenhaver company, 2d Battalion of Riflemen, of Lancaster county, commanded by Colonel GREEN, the five following men, viz.

Balizer Baumgartner, about 32 years of age, 5 feet 10 inches high, well set, sandy coloured hair; had on a green frock and trowsers; took his arms and accoutrements with him.

Adam Baumgartner, brother of the said Balizer, about 30 years of age, near 5 feet 10 inches high, black hair; had on a green frock and trowsers.

Adam Titler, about 20 years of age, 5 feet 10 inches high, stoops in his walk, sandy coloured hair; had on a green frock and trowsers; took his arms and accoutrements with him.

Jacob Musser, about 20 years of age, near 5 feet 8 inches high, a Shoemaker by trade; had on a green frock and trowsers.

John Dubbs, about 25 years of age, 5 feet 2 inches high, well set, black hair; had on a green frock and trowsers; was Drummer to the company.

They were all of Hanover township, Lancaster county, neighbours to each other, had all received the advance money – The said Balizer Baumgartner had entered in the place of another man, who paid him Ten Pounds for the same. – The amrs and accoutrements were appraised in order to be paid for by the public. Whoever takes up said deserters, and delivers them at the camp, at Amboy, or secures them, so that they may be delivered to the Commanding Officers of said Battalion, shall receive for the said Balizer Baumgartner, the reward of Twenty four Dollars, and for each of the others Eight Dollars, and all reasonable charges, paid by THOMAS COPENHAVER, Captain.

Index

H

J

K

L

M

Machir, Alexander 80
Mapping, John 8
Mark, Conrad 72
Marstellar, P. 72
Marsteller, P. 38, 73
Marsteller, Philip 27
Meily, Jacob 45
Miles, Samuel 79, 80
Miller, John Conrad 37
Miller, Michael 8
Mohn, Viola K 12
Mohn, Viola K. 47

N

Nach, Henry 49

O

Orth, Adam 27, 28, 29, 30, 31, 69, 77
Orth, Balthaser 35, 36, 69, 75
Orth, Baltzer 28, 77
Orth, Balzer 33
Orth, Catherine 77
Orth, Godlove S. 34
Orth, Gottlieb 75
Orth, Johannes 69
Orth, John 77
Orth, Rosina Kucher ii, 33

P

Peiffer, Jacob 72
Penn, William ii
Pickens, Andrew 60
Preston, William 59, 61
Putnam, Israel 16

www.ingramcontent.com/pod-product-compliance
Lightning Source LLC
Chambersburg PA
CBHW070813270326
41927CB00010B/2400